T0330824

ROUTLEDGE LIBRARY EDITIONS:
SOVIET ECONOMICS

Volume 12

THE SECOND FIVE-YEAR PLAN OF DEVELOPMENT OF THE U.S.S.R.

THE SECOND FIVE-YEAR PLAN OF DEVELOPMENT OF THE U.S.S.R.

W.P. COATES
and
ZELDA K. COATES

Routledge
Taylor & Francis Group

LONDON AND NEW YORK

First published in 1934 by Methuen & Co. Ltd.

This edition first published in 2023
by Routledge
4 Park Square, Milton Park, Abingdon, Oxon OX14 4RN

and by Routledge
605 Third Avenue, New York, NY 10158

Routledge is an imprint of the Taylor & Francis Group, an informa business

© 1934

British Library Cataloguing in Publication Data
A catalogue record for this book is available from the British Library

ISBN: 978-1-032-48466-2 (Set)
ISBN: 978-1-032-48749-6 (Volume 12) (hbk)
ISBN: 978-1-032-48753-3 (Volume 12) (pbk)
ISBN: 978-1-003-39058-9 (Volume 12) (ebk)

DOI: 10.4324/9781003390589

Publisher's Note
The publisher has gone to great lengths to ensure the quality of this reprint but points out that some imperfections in the original copies may be apparent.

Disclaimer
The publisher has made every effort to trace copyright holders and would welcome correspondence from those they have been unable to trace.

THE SECOND
FIVE-YEAR PLAN
OF DEVELOPMENT OF THE
U. S. S. R.

by W. P. COATES
and ZELDA K. COATES

With a Preface by the Rt. Hon.
HERBERT S. MORRISON, L.C.C.
And a Foreword by
A. OZERSKY
Chairman, Trade Delegation of the U.S.S.R. in London

1934
METHUEN & CO. LTD. LONDON
36 Essex Street W.C.

First published in 1934

PRINTED IN GREAT BRITAIN

PREFACE

I SHALL not be expected to identify myself with the political system of government in Soviet Russia nor with the doctrines of the Communist International, with whose section in this country I have had considerable controversy. Nor am I obliged to agree with the whole of Russia's economic policy.

The efforts of Soviet Russia, however, to evolve a plan of economy on a collectivist basis is one of the most interesting and important contributions to the practical handling of modern industrial problems. The Soviet Government, in applying the principles of public ownership and management to the extent it considers to be practicable, is conducting the greatest economic experiment of our time over a vast territory inhabited by a huge population.

Students of the disgraceful disease of poverty amidst plenty, which characterizes all capitalist countries, including Fascist countries, cannot but be deeply interested in Russian economic affairs. During my own visit to Russia in 1933 I was greatly impressed by the real effort which is being made by the Soviet Government and its local organs to give to Russia the advantages of a planned collectivist economic system.

Certain phases of Russia's economic administration are, of course, open to criticism. Perhaps the political system is partly responsible for some of the defects. On the admission of important leaders of the Communist Party in Russia there are still serious imperfections in management. Whilst it is no excuse for inefficiency we, who are not Russians, must remember that Russia is relatively new to modern large-scale economic enterprise, and that the industrial psychology of the masses of the Russian people is not yet attuned to that of the hurry and skurry of western economic life.

During recent years, however, great changes have taken place in the industrial life of Russia, and it is well that we should all be as familiar with these things as is possible.

The present volume aims at a survey of the Second Five-Year Plan. I can take no responsibility for its accuracy or its opinions, but it has been 'vetted' by responsible Russian authorities and it claims to be an exposition of, at any rate, the semi-official Russian view of the second Five-Year Plan. It should be a volume well worthy of study. But students of modern economic problems must think and judge for themselves on the first-class issues of economic policy involved.

HERBERT MORRISON

FOREWORD

WORK in connexion with the carrying out of the Second Five-Year Plan is at present in full swing. Elaborate details of its estimates have been published in several lengthy volumes in the U.S.S.R., but they, unfortunately, are for the most part inaccessible to the English reader.

The summary of the achievements of the First Five-Year Plan and the provisions of the Second Five-Year Plan contained in this book has been compiled very carefully by the authors, despite the difficulty of compressing it into this brief review.

In recommending this book to the British public, I would also like to lay stress on the very great importance of the people of this country obtaining a knowledge of what is being done in the Soviet Union and the aims of its Government.

In the first place, we can all learn something from one another, however sharply we may disagree on matters of policy, and even of ideals. We in the U.S.S.R. have always been willing to learn from the great industrial progress of Great Britain, the U.S.A., and other countries, and it may be that the U.S.S.R., with its new organization, new aims, and rapid development can have something to teach other countries too.

Above all, however, do I welcome this book, because by spreading knowledge of what we are doing in our country, by familiarizing the British people with our purpose and plans, it will, we may hope, help very considerably in strengthening the bonds between our two peoples and thus help to consolidate peace.

A. OZERSKY

CONTENTS

MAPS

MEANING OF RUSSIAN TERMS USED IN TEXT

Donbas . . Donetz River Basin.

Goelro . . The 1920 Soviet Electrification Plan.

Gosplan . . State Planning Commission.

Kolkhoz . . Peasant Collective Farm.

Kolkhozy . . Peasant Collective Farms.

Kulak . . Rich Profiteering Peasant (literally ' fist ').

Machine Tractor Stations . State organization for the supply of machinery and agranomic aid generally to the peasantry, particularly to the Kolkhozy.

Piatiletka . . Five-Year Plan.

Sovkhoz . . Soviet State Farm.

Sovkhozy . . Soviet State Farms.

1926–7 PRICES

The estimation of the value of goods in 1926–7 prices is calculated by Soviet economists in order that they may have a strictly comparable measure of the actual volume of production.

No purchases or sales are made at 1926–7 prices.

Each enterprise supplies to the Central Statistical Authorities a return of the value of each class of goods it has manufactured at actual prices, and also of the value calculated in the 1926–7 prices as fixed by the Gosplan of the U.S.S.R. It is thus possible to see at a glance whether and what progress has been made.

1926–7 is taken as a basic year, because this was the year when the restoration of Soviet industry was completed.

WEIGHTS AND MEASURES

CENTNER (The Russian Centner is
             what is generally known
             as a double centner) $= 220.46$ lb.

CUBIC METRE   .   .   .   . $= 35.315$ cubic feet.

KILOGRAM .   .   .   .   . $= 2.2046$ lb.

KILOMETRE.   .   .   .   . $= 0.621$ mile.

METRE   .   .   .   .   . $= 39.37$ inches.

HECTARE   .   .   .   .   . $= 2.471$ acres.

ROUBLE $= 100$ Kopeks   .   .   . $= 2$s. 0d. @ par.

SQUARE METRE   .   .   . $= 10.76$ square feet.

Federated Republics & Areas of EUROPEAN RUSSIA

Kola

Karelia

Leningrad
Leningrad Area

White Russia

Kiev

Kharkov

Ukraine

Odessa

Crimea

Western Area

Moscow
Moscow A.

Ivanovo

Central Area

Northern Area

Gorkovski

Chuvash

Saratov A.

Stalingrad Area

N. Caucasus

Volga-German

Kalmyk A.

Dagestan

Transcaucas.n Fed.n

Zyryan Area

URALS

Sverdlovsk Area

Obsk-Irtysh Area

Chelyabinsk Area

Tatar

Bashkiria

Middle Volga

Kazakstan

Turkmenistan

J.F.H.

0   250   500   Miles   1000

INTRODUCTION

IN the following pages we give a brief summary of the results of the First Five-Year Plan and the estimates for the Second Five-Year Plan. The interest and importance of this subject need scarcely be stressed.

In spite of all the incredulity of the opponents and even some would-be friends of the U.S.S.R., in spite of the jeers and prophecies of failure, the fundamental successes so far achieved have been so striking, so spectacular, that they have compelled the unwilling admiration even of many of those who, by their class position and training, are most hostile to the Soviet system.

Thus the foreign Editor of the *News Chronicle* summed up the result of the First Five-Year Plan as follows :

> ' Despite all difficulties, the actual record of the achievement under the Plan is astounding. Chief among the objectives of the Plan was to provide Russia with a heavy industry. At the end of little more than four years she finds herself in possession of new industrial plants that include some of the most powerful in the world. They number nearly eight hundred, spread all over the vast national territory—the great motor and ball-bearing works at Moscow, the Ford motor works at Nizhni-Novgorod, tractor plants at Kharkov and Rostov, the Bereznikov Chemical Combine, immense engineering works in the Urals, and the great dam and electricity undertakings at Dnieperstroi.'
>
> *[News Chronicle, December* 30, 1932]

And even the *Morning Post*, although making the most of the temporary difficulties, was constrained to admit :

> ' It would, nevertheless, be hazardous to assume off-hand that the Five-Year Plan has been a failure.

We are too near to the event and too ill-supplied with reliable information to pass any confident judgment ; but from certain aspects it has quite evidently been at least a partial success. The plan was an extremely ambitious undertaking, which was bound to place an immense psychological strain on the human material. Yet the collapse of the whole Soviet system which was many times predicted has not occurred. Stalin may have tottered on occasion, but he is still there, and the system too. Moreover, if the achievement has lagged behind the estimates, that may be because the estimates were placed impossibly high for the deliberate purpose of stimulating effort. After making every allowance for exaggerated Soviet statistics and for low quality of output, it still remains that as much industrial plant has been laid down in four years and three months as would normally have occupied the best part of a generation. Again, the programme of peasant " collectivisation " has been substantially carried through, however disappointing the immediate effects upon the output of agriculture. So much must be acknowledged in any sober appreciation of performance under the Plan.'

[*Morning Post, January* 3, 1933]

And now we hear more and more both at home and abroad of the advisability of drafting Five-Year Plans for this or that branch of the national economy.

For a Government which set out to reorganize their country on a Socialist basis, the planning of the national economy was, of course, an absolute necessity.

Accordingly we find that as early as 1920, when foreign intervention was still going strong and when the financial and economic blockade against Soviet Russia was still at its height, a special committee met under the chairmanship of G. Krzhizhanovsky, who afterwards became head of the State Planning Commission (Gosplan), and at the instruction of the Soviet Government drew up a fifteen-years' plan of electrification of Soviet Russia as a basis for its future industrialization and economic development.

This plan, known as the 'Goelro,' provided for the construction of a great system of electrical power plants with an aggregate capacity of 1,750,000 kws., with the necessary transmission lines.

At that time even the few existing pre-revolutionary power plants were either shut down or only operating partially. Consequently, like the subsequent Five-Year Plans—the 'Goelro,' too, was derided as Utopian.

But already by 1927–8, i.e. in seven years, the capacity of the stations in operation was 1,792,000 kws., with an output of 5,160,000,000 kw. hours as against an output of 1,945,000,000 kw. hours in 1913. This progress was a sufficient reply to those who thought (and hoped) that the Bolshevik Government would founder when they came to attempt the economic construction of the country.

In 1925, when the process of the restoration of the pre-war national economy was nearing completion, the Gosplan began to draft one year control figures for the development of the national economy generally. These estimates or control figures corresponded, on the whole, remarkably closely with the actual results obtained in large-scale industry.

In agriculture, however, which was at that time organized mainly on privately worked small peasant farms (there were actually 25,000,000 of such farms in 1927–8), the control figures fell pretty wide of the mark.

It was obviously impossible to plan ahead for small individual farming with their primitive means of production, their varying capacities and their dependence on natural forces entirely outside their control.

In 1927, having gained experience with the working of the 'Goelro' and the annual estimates, the Soviet authorities undertook the more ambitious task of planning the whole national economy—industry, agriculture, transport, trade, &c.—as well as the development of the cultural life of the country for five years ahead. At the same time, understanding that agricultural progress could only then be planned if it was organized on a large scale State or collective basis, the First Five-Year Plan for agriculture sought in the first instance to bring about such collectivization at the earliest possible moment.

The Plan at first drafted erred on the side of over-

Federated Republics & Areas of ASIATIC RUSSIA

EUROPEAN

•Moscow

RUSSIA

ARCTIC CIRCLE

Sverdlovsk Area

Obsk-Irtysh Area

Yenisei

Chelyabinsk A.

R. Ob

Siberian Area

K a z a k s t a n

Tomsk

•Kuznetsk

Semipalatinsk

Irku

Turkmenist'n

Uzbekistan

Kirghiz

Tajikistan

| 0 | 500 | 1000 | 2000 |

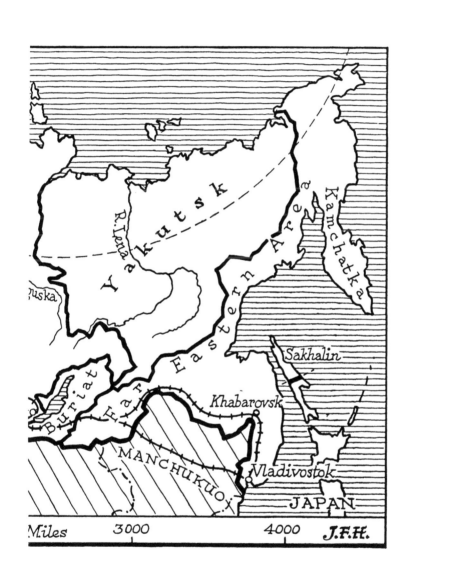

Miles   3000   4000   *J.F.H.*

caution. Two variants were laid down, a maximum and a minimum, and the latter was at first adopted as a basis. But when in 1929, the Plan was discussed at the Soviet Congress of the U.S.S.R., the minimum variant was definitely rejected and the maximum variant was fixed as the basis. Subsequently, the Plan as a whole was completed in four and a quarter years, and although in some branches this maximum variant was not quite fulfilled in many other branches of the national economy even the maximum figures were exceeded.

The Second Five-Year Plan continues the aim of the First Five-Year Plan, i.e. of organizing the work and life of the country on the basis of a planned national economy. But, as a result of the success of the First Five-Year Plan, the Second Five-Year Plan covers even a larger field.

There is no need to deal with the estimates and aims of the Second Five-Year Plan, these will be found in subsequent pages. We would only draw attention here to two of the general aims of the Plan which are discussed and attacked from time to time, e.g. firstly, to strengthen the defensive capacity of the Soviet Union, and secondly, to transform her into one of the most technically advanced countries in the world and to make her economically and technically independent.

The fear has often been expressed that when once the U.S.S.R. has built up her economy and is independent of the rest of the world, she will cease to be a customer, but will become a serious competitor in foreign markets. Such fears betray an amazing ignorance of history, of the mechanism of foreign trade, and of the principles underlying the Soviet Socialist system of economy.

In the first place, it is well known that, for instance, Germany became a far better customer for the goods of other countries, including those of Great Britain, after her industrial development, than she had ever been before. Similarly, the U.S.A., the most highly industrialized country in the world, which, at a pinch, could be completely self-supporting, is not only an exporter, but also an importer of a large variety of goods. Why should the U.S.S.R. be an exception to this rule ?

A higher standard of living for the people, such as the Soviet planned economy aims at, gives rise to ever-new demands for all kinds of goods of both home and foreign produce.

When the Soviet leaders speak of making the U.S.S.R. economically and technically independent, they do not, of course, mean that they wish to cut off the U.S.S.R. economically from the rest of the world; what they desire, is to be in a position of equality when bargaining with other countries; that they should no longer be in a position because of their weak industrial development to have to agree to whatever onerous terms in trade and other agreements that other countries may try to impose; that they should be in a position to pick and choose their markets like other countries; as M. Rosengoltz, Commissar for Foreign Trade of the U.S.S.R. said in a speech delivered April 23, 1933:

> 'Generally speaking, we would have no such urgent necessity to import, we are no longer so dependent on foreign markets. Our hands are now untied. We are now able to extend or limit our imports in accordance with the terms offered us abroad, and also in accordance with our trade and political relations with the various countries in which our orders can be placed.
>
> 'During our Second Five-Year Plan, we shall not extend our imports unless we get very much better credit terms. . . . We shall also take into account the way in which this or that country treats our exports and whether we have normal trading relations in a given country.
>
> 'If all these factors are favourable we could extend our imports to such a degree that we might become a considerable factor in the economy of the country with which we do trade. If, on the other hand, these factors are unfavourable we shall, of course, limit our imports.'

And in a more recent speech delivered at the Congress of the Communist Party of the U.S.S.R., he said:

> 'What is our policy in regard to the placing of orders abroad? We are not in favour of autarchy,

but we shall not purchase any large quantity of goods unless the conditions for the purchase of such goods are radically changed and improved.'

As for exporting without importing, what need would the U.S.S.R. have to export if it did not import goods ? The mere accumulation of gold is not an object in itself even in capitalist countries, still less in a Socialist country, where there is no private profit-making and whose citizens neither would nor could make foreign investments.   If the U.S.S.R. required no imports, then it stands to reason she would necessarily cease to export.

Being economically and technically independent, above all, signifies for the U.S.S.R. a feeling of safety in case of an attack by other Powers.   In case of an emergency, if blockaded on one or more frontiers, she might have to do without luxuries, but she would have the necessities within her own borders.

And this brings us to the other important aim of the Second Five-Year Plan mentioned above—to strengthen her defensive power.

During the First Five-Year Plan, the U.S.S.R. had succeeded in building up a powerful, well-equipped Red Army and Red Air Force, and she is continuing to strengthen these forces during the Second Five-Year Plan. For this she is often attacked as militarist.   Perhaps we cannot do better than quote the reply made by Mr. R. J. Boothby, M.P., to the Duchess of Atholl on this very point :

> ' She blamed the Soviet Government almost violently for arming and boasting over the wireless that they possess a more efficient army and air force than they have had for two or three years.   I would only say to her that if she were a citizen of Russia and found herself in existing circumstances between Japan on the one side and Germany on the other, she would think it wise to possess a certain amount of armaments.   I do not think that we can make that kind of case against the Soviet Government.
>
> ' I do not believe that they are militant, but I am not at all sure that the military strength, particularly

the air strength, of the Soviet Government during the last twelve months has not been a factor for peace throughout the world. At any rate, I think the situation of the world is sufficiently dangerous, as far as they are concerned, to make it difficult for us to throw stones at them for possessing armaments.'

[*Hansard, March* 1, 1934, *col.* 1390]

We would further recall here that the U.S.S.R. has given an earnest of its desire for peace and disarmament by proposing complete universal disarmament, and when this was rejected by the other Powers, the Soviet representative proposed an immediate, simultaneous reduction of all the armaments of the big Powers (including the U.S.S.R.) by 50 per cent.

This, too, was rejected. In view of this rejection, in view, too, of her still vivid memory of the ravages of foreign intervention on her soil and of the frankly hostile attitude of Japan in the East and Germany in the West, the Five-Year Plan naturally provides for a considerable strengthening of her defensive forces.

Like the First Five-Year Plan, so the Second Five-Year Plan was based on the detailed material supplied by the local economic authorities and the local Gosplans throughout the Soviet Union, and each section of the Plan was worked out by the corresponding experts within the All-Union State Planning Commission.

Practically the whole of the scientific forces of the country participated in the drafting of the Second Five-Year Plan—the Academy of Science of the U.S.S.R., 200 various scientific research institutions and many well-known Soviet scientists, including over 300 specialists in various branches of science and technique.

Some fifteen All-Union Conferences were held to discuss various questions and separate sections of the draft plan. The Plan was also widely discussed at workers' meetings and conferences, and in the press, and finally it was discussed very fully at the Congress of the Communist Party of the U.S.S.R., January–February 1934, when the final figures were adopted.

Of course, the Plan covers such a wide field and such a vast area that readjustments, whether in an upward or downward direction, may be necessary from time to time, but the results of 1933—the first year of the Second Five-Year Plan—and still more those of the first six months of 1934 undoubtedly augur well for the realization, in the main, of the whole of the Second Piatiletka, ambitious though it may be.

The facts and figures given in the following pages have been compiled entirely from official Soviet publications.

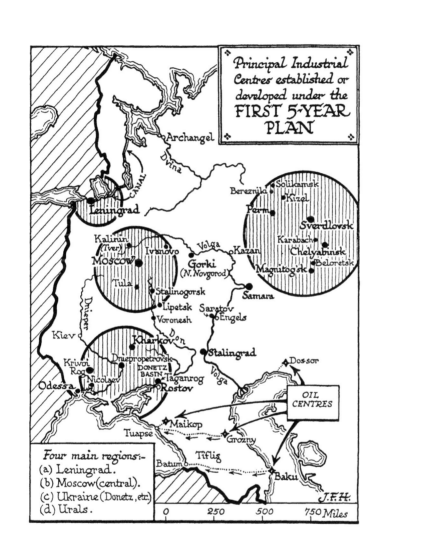

Principal Industrial Centres established or developed under the FIRST 5-YEAR PLAN

Archangel

Dvina

CANAL

Leningrad

Bereznila • Solikamsk
• Kizel
Perm

Sverdlovsk

Karabach •
Chelyabinsk •
Magnitogsk • • Beloretsk

Kalinin
(Tver)
Moscow
Ivanovo • Volga
Kazan
Gorki
(N. Novgorod)
Tula
Stalinogorsk
Samara
Lipetsk Saratov
Voronesh Engels
Dnieper
Kiev
Kharkov
Don
Stalingrad
Kriwoi
Rog Dniepropetrovsk
DONETZ
Nicolaev BASIN Taganrog
Odessa Rostov

Dossor

OIL
CENTRES

Maikop
Tuapse Grozny
Tiflis
Batum
Baku

J.F.H.

Four main regions:—
(a) Leningrad.
(b) Moscow (central).
(c) Ukraine (Donetz, etc)
(d) Urals.

0   250   500   750 Miles

I

SUMMARY OF RESULTS OF FIRST FIVE-YEAR PLAN

THE FIRST FIVE-YEAR PLAN

(SUMMARY OF RESULTS)

THE First Five-Year Plan was the first definite attempt to plan the development of the national economy and also the cultural development of a huge country in accordance with its possibilities, its natural resources, and the needs of its population.

The Plan originally drawn up was for the five economic years from October 1, 1928, to September 30, 1933, and the work was started in accordance with the Plan in October 1928.

Although it had been generally agreed that the Plan, even as it stood, provided for a rate of development unprecedented in the economic history of any country, nevertheless, the success attained in the fulfilment of the Plan during the first two years was such that it was decided to speed up the work so as to fulfil it within four years and three months. In addition, as the work proceeded the plans were revised usually in an upward direction, and it was decided to construct a number of new enterprises not envisaged in the original Plan.

Among the supplementary constructions carried out during the First Piatiletka, but not originally included in the latter, the following may be mentioned. The construction of a coal and metallurgical base in the East, the construction of the industrial giants : the Kharkov Tractor Works, the Saratov Combine Harvester Works, the Gorky (formerly Nizhni-Novgorod), Turret Lathe Works, the Milling Machine-Tool Works in Moscow, the Moscow Watch Factory, the Azovstal and New Tula Steel Works, the Nikopol and Pervo-Uralsk Tube-rolling Works, the Synthetic Rubber Works, the opening up of the Karaganda coal district, the discovery and exploitation of the Khibin Apatite deposits, &c.

Further, there has been the organization of new industries, such as the manufacture of combine harvesters, caterpillar tractors, cotton pickers, and similar machines for other crops, 50,000 kw. turbines, electric cars, powerful locomotives, blooming mills. and complex equipment for the iron and steel industry, rotary printing presses and linotypes, complex, optical, and measuring instruments, powerful radio transmitters, super-hard alloys, &c.

Moreover, during this period and supplementary to the Plan, Soviet industry succeeded in solving on an industrial scale some most complicated technical problems, such as the production of vanadium from Kerch and Ural ores, of ferro-alloys, various types of special steel, the selective flotations from poly-metallic ores, the production of aluminium and synthetic rubber, the utilization of inferior types of fuel, the extensive electrification and large-scale application of chemistry to production processes, &c.

During 1930, the economic year, which ran from October 1 of one year to September 30 of the following year, was replaced by the calendar year and the last quarter (October to December) of 1930, was declared a 'special quarter.' This meant that, in the main, the Five-Year Plan was to be carried out in four years and a quarter, i.e. it was to be completed by December 31, 1932, instead of September 30, 1933.

Aim of Plan.

The fundamental aim of the Plan was to lay the foundations of the establishment of a classless Socialist society in the U.S.S.R. by : (1) the development of a large-scale industry both of producers' (means of production) and consumers' goods ; (2) the introduction of large-scale agriculture based on modern technique ; (3) raising enormously the cultural level of the country.

To attain these aims it was necessary in the first place to develop the heavy industries, to organize large-scale agriculture by the establishment of State and peasant collective farms, and to provide the country, as far as possible, with a supply of home raw products for industry by the extension on a large scale of the area under industrial plants such as cotton, flax, &c.

In accordance with the objects stated above, we find that the outstanding feature of the result of the First Five-Year Plan is the industrialization of the U.S.S.R., although, as we shall see below, important progress has also been made in agriculture.

The proportion of planned [1] industrial goods in the total output of the country has risen from 48 per cent. in 1927–8 to 70 per cent. in 1932.

Similarly of the total large-scale (census [2]) industrial output, in 1932, 52·5 per cent. were heavy industrial goods as compared with 44·3 per cent. of the total industrial output in 1927–8. (The Five-Year Plan had fixed the proportion for 1932–3 at 47·5 per cent. of the total output.)

The value of the total output of the census industries in 1932 was 34·3 milliard roubles (1926–7 prices) as compared with 36·6 milliard roubles fixed for 1932–3 in the Five-Year Plan, i.e. 93·7 per cent. of the whole Piatiletka was carried out in the four and a quarter years. *The volume of large-scale industrial output in 1932 was 218·5 per cent. of the industrial output of 1928, and 334·5 per cent. of the output of 1913.*

The output of the means of production in 1932 exceeded that of the Five-Year Plan for 1932–3 by 3·4 per cent., the output of the heavy industries alone was 9·6 per cent. in excess of the Plan. Compared with 1928, the output of the means of production increased 2·6 fold and compared with the pre-war period 4·2 fold.

On the other hand, the output of consumers' goods in 1932 was only 84·9 per cent. of that fixed in the Plan for 1932–3, nevertheless, the output of such goods was 187·3 per cent. of 1928, and 273·5 per cent. of the output of the corresponding industries in 1913.

---

[1] *Planned industry* includes all plants and factories controlled by the four People's Commissariats—People's Commissariat of Heavy Industry, People's Commissariat of Light Industry, People's Commissariat of Timber and People's Commissariat of Supply. The Commissariat of Supply has recently been abolished, and in its place a Commissariat for Home Trade and a Food Commissariat have been set up.

[2] *Census industry* comprises industrial enterprises employing not less than sixteen workers where there is mechanical driving power, and not less than thirty workers where there is no mechanical driving power.

Change in Geographical Distribution of Industry.

Apart from the great increase in the output of industry perhaps the most remarkable change brought about by the Five-Year Plan was that of the geographical distribution of industry.

In pre-revolutionary Russia, three-fourths of the industry of the whole country was concentrated in four districts of European Russia, e.g. Moscow, Ivanovo, St. Petersburg (now Leningrad), and the Ukraine, and it was part of the settled policy of Tsardom to prevent the economic and cultural development of the outlying regions. Siberia, Central Asia, the Caucasus, and Transcaucasia, for instance, were in the position of economically and culturally backward primitive colonies of Central Russia. In these regions there were no large-scale industries, very inadequate railways, practically no industrial working-class.

As one example of the way in which the Soviet authorities have stimulated the development of the national economy of the districts inhabited by the national minorities, the North Caucasian Area may be cited.

During the First Five-Year Plan, the capital invested in the whole North Caucasian Area was twice that of the total amount of the basic capital at the beginning of the plan. But in the regions of the national minorities of the North Caucasian Area the amount invested was four times as great.

Similarly, over the whole of the U.S.S.R., during the Five-Year Plan, 48 per cent. of the capital investments was used for new constructions (52 per cent. was invested in the development of existing factories). In Middle Asia, however, 80 per cent. of investments went into new concerns. In Uzbekistan, during the last four years, sixty-five factories were constructed.

The Five-Year Plan and the supplementary decisions of the Government respecting the industrial development of the Eastern areas of the Soviet Union set out to make an end to this neglect of the rich resources of the outlying districts of the U.S.S.R. It sought to bring about a more even distribution of industry over the whole country, shifting the industries nearer to the sources of the raw materials, to eliminate the economic and cultural backwardness of the numerous national minorities and at the same time to strengthen the defensive capacity of the Soviet Union.

The economic development of the rich natural resources of the various national Republics and districts would also relieve the transport system of the country of the necessity to carry considerable freights of raw materials, &c., from one part of the Soviet Union to another.

Whilst by no means neglecting to reconstruct, extend, and develop the existing industrial works, and to build new industries in the European parts of the U.S.S.R., it was definitely decided to assure a still higher rate of industrialization and of general economic and cultural development for the hitherto more backward districts.

As a result of the industrialization of the areas inhabited by the national minorities, the number of workers has increased proportionately more rapidly among the national minorities than in the U.S.S.R. as a whole.

The almost inexhaustible deposits of coal in the Kuznetz basin, Karaganda, and other districts, the iron ore of the Urals and Siberia, the deposits of non-ferrous metals in Kazakstan and Central Asia which are of world importance, the immensely valuable sources of water power, the vast expanses of forest, the newly discovered oil beds, and the numerous resources of useful minerals, formed a natural basis for the movement of industry towards the East.

These natural resources, which before had been known only in their rough outlines, were discovered in greater quantities and prepared for industrial exploitation by widespread geological surveys and research work during the First Five-Year Plan period.

A New Coal Metallurgical Base.

As a result, a new coal and metallurgical base was established in the East for the exploitation of the huge coal and ore deposits of the Urals and Siberia. The ascertained geological resources of iron ore in these regions were estimated by the beginning of 1932 at 635,000,000 tons of potential metal. The resources of coal for industrial exploitation which have been discovered in the Urals, Western Siberia, and Karaganda (Kazakstan) have been estimated at 9·5 milliard tons, while the total geological resources of these regions have been estimated at 450 milliard tons.   These figures, which do not comprise the vast resources of coal deposits of Eastern Siberia and the Far Eastern territory or the deposits of iron ore in the Far East and the Middle Volga region, give some idea of the tremendous prospects which are opened up in connexion with the industrial exploitation of the national resources of the eastern districts.

The construction and the setting into operation of the first units of the Magnitogorsk and Kuznetsk metallurgical plants, and the reconstruction of the metallurgical industry of the Urals has already given a more even territorial distribution of the iron and steel industry.   The share of the eastern regions in the total output of pig iron in the U.S.S.R. has risen from 21·4 per cent. in 1928 to 25 per cent. in 1932.

Great prospecting and constructional work was also carried out in the coal-metallurgical districts of the South of the U.S.S.R.—the Krivoy Rog and Kerch as well as in the iron Basin of the Kursk Magnetic Anomaly.

Coal.

Before the War, only the coal resources of the Donetz were being exploited on anything like a large scale, and yet 70 per cent. of the total coal resources suitable for industrial exploitation is concentrated in the Urals and Siberia, including over 60 per cent. in the Kuzbas.   Such districts as Kazakstan, which possesses ascertained resources of coal for industrial exploitation amounting to milliards of tons, Central Asia, the Moscow basin, the coal deposits of Transcaucasia, of the northern districts of the U.S.S.R. and of many other regions had remained almost untouched prior to the Revolution, and did not attain any great significance until the First Five-Year Plan period.

By the end of this period, the Soviet Union already had seven large coal-producing regions, e.g. Donbas, Kuzbas, Karaganda, Chelyabinsk, Kizel, Cheremkhovo, and the Moscow basin.   The Kuzbas region increased its output from 878,000 tons in 1913 to 2,500,000 tons in 1927–8 and 7,300,000 tons in 1932, i.e. the output has been almost trebled during the Five-Year Plan period.

Karaganda has grown into an important coal region ; in 1932 it was already yielding 723,000 tons of coal, with great prospects of further development. A large increase in the output of coal is to be noted in the Far East, in the Cheremkhovo basin, in the Moscow basin, in Tkvarcheli, and in other regions.

In the course of the First Piatiletka, great work was done in modernizing and mechanizing the mining and haulage of coal. The mechanization of coal cutting rose from 15·7 per cent. in 1927–8 to 63·6 per cent. by the end of the Five-Year Plan period.

The type of the pits has changed radically. In the period preceding that of the First Five-Year Plan, the output of the largest pits did not exceed 500,000 to 600,000 tons ; now the new pits in the main regions are capable of producing 1,000,000 tons and more each, per annum.

The output of coal in 1932 was 64,320,000 tons, as compared with 29,040,000 tons in 1913 and 35,220,000 tons in 1927–8. (According to the Five-Year Plan, the output in 1932–3 should have been 75,000,000 tons.)

Oil.

Substantial changes have been made during the Five-Year Plan period in the geographical distribution of the oil industry, which before the Revolution was concentrated entirely in the Baku and Grozny districts. Enormous work was accomplished both before and particularly during the Five-Year Plan period in reconstructing and developing the oil industry in the latter areas.

In addition, toward the end of the First Five-Year Plan period, oil extraction was begun in a number of new regions, which, due to their rich deposits, offer great prospects of industrial development (Maikop, the Urals, Sterlitamak, Georgia, Ukhta, &c.), and in the newly developed districts where oil extraction played only an insignificant part up to the beginning of the Five-Year Plan period (Emba, Turkmenistan, Saghalien).

Together with the organization of oil extraction in a

number of new regions, a network of oil-pipe lines has been
built : Baku-Batum, Grozny-Tuapse, the pipe line for
oil products from Armavir to Trudovaya, as well as a
number of oil-refining plants in the main regions requiring
oil products. These measures have introduced radical
changes in the territorial distribution of the oil industry.

The radical reconstruction of the technical processes
of extraction and refining of oil ensured the fulfilment of
the Five-Year Plan for oil in two and a half years. In
1932, the output of oil and gas was 22,270,000 tons as
compared with 21,700,000 tons set by the Five-Year Plan
for the last year of the Plan, and only 9,230,000 tons in
1913. The plan for oil refining was likewise over-fulfilled.
In 1932 the output of refined oil amounted to 20,000,000
tons as compared with 19,100,000 tons set by the Plan.
As a result of the work done during the Five-Year Plan
period, the oil industry of the U.S.S.R. rose to second place
in the world.

*Over 90 per cent. of the oil now produced in the oilfields of
the U.S.S.R. is obtained from wells drilled by the Soviets after
the nationalization of the industry.*

Other Fuels.

As regards other fuels, 13,550,000 tons of dark oil was
produced as compared with 12,540,000 tons laid down in
the Plan for 1932–3, and 6,680,000 tons produced in 1913.
About 80,000,000 cubic metres of wood fuel was prepared
in 1932 as compared with the Plan of 59,800,000 cubic
metres for 1932–3, and 68,000,000 cubic metres in 1913.
The output of peat for industrial purposes was 13,302,000
tons in 1932 as compared with the Plan of 12,300,000 tons
in 1932–3, and 1,690,000 tons in 1913.

In addition, the development of the extraction of oil
shale on industrial lines began during the First Five-Year
Plan period. During this period three new mines were put
into operation with a total capacity of about 1,700,000
tons, 320,000 tons being produced in 1932.

During the First Five-Year Plan period, the fuel supply
of the country has been radically reorganised and put on a
solid foundation. The big successes attending the development of the fuel industry, as well as the creation of a home

machine building base for the fuel industry in the course of the Piatiletka ensure the further development of the power resources of the Soviet Union to the extent required for the completion of the technical reconstruction of the economy of the country as a whole in the course of the Second Piatiletka.

Metallurgical Industry.

By the beginning of the First Piatiletka, there were sixty-nine blast furnaces working in the U.S.S.R., having a total volume of 20,000 cubic metres. In the course of the Five-Year Plan period, three blast furnaces were abandoned, four discontinued work for a long period while undergoing radical reconstruction, seventeen new ones were built, whilst a number of blast furnaces which were not operating were set going again, involving in almost all cases considerable reconstruction and modernization.

Thus, by January 1, 1933, there were 102 blast furnaces working in the U.S.S.R., with a total volume of 36,800 cubic metres.

Eleven blast furnaces, out of the seventeen new ones, represent powerful, fully mechanized units, not inferior in equipment to the best American blast furnaces.

The U.S.S.R. formerly had no pig-casting machines, but at the end of the Five-Year Plan period, twelve such machines had already been installed.

At the beginning of the Five-Year Plan period, 202 open hearth furnaces were working, with a total hearth area of 4,630 square metres. By the end of the Five-Year Plan period, there were 265 furnaces with a total hearth area of 6,421 square metres.

Almost all the newly built open hearth furnaces are mechanized, having charging machines and powerful ladle cranes.

The existing rolling mills were completely reconstructed during the Five-Year Plan period, and eleven new mills were constructed.

Considerable progress has been made in the mechanization of various operations, and new branches of metallurgy, such as electro-metallurgy, have been introduced. The factory ' Electrostal,' from a small experimental factory, has now grown into a giant first-class metallurgical works, and in 1932 2·1 per cent. of the total steel output in the country was electro-steel (in the U.S.A. this proportion is only 1·5 per cent. ; in Germany, 1·2 per cent). A variety of important alloys and high-grade steels are now produced, the output of high-grade steel now being seven times that in 1928.

Owing to the shortage of skilled workers and the difficulties necessarily experienced by workers and young engineers used to primitive methods of work in mastering the new modern technique, the output of the metal industry failed to reach the figures laid down for it in the Five-Year Plan, but the output in 1932 was above that in 1913, and very considerably above that in 1927–8 as the following table indicates :

OUTPUT 1,000 TONS

	1927–8.	1932.	Five-Year Plan for 1932–3.
Pig-iron	3,283	6,173	10,000
Steel	4,251	5,922	10,300
Rolled steel . . .	3,408	4,289	8,000
Pipe and tubing . . .	171	309	—

It should be borne in mind that the metals industry, like the coal, oil, and many other industries, had come practically to a standstill in 1920, as a result of the world and civil wars, foreign intervention, and blockade.[1]

Electrification.

The Five-Year Plan for electrification was not completed by the end of 1932, but the enormous progress made can be gauged from the fact that in 1913 there was no station with higher power than 25,000 kws.

In 1929 the most powerful station was of 75,000 kws.

In 1932 there were ten stations with power ranging from 100,000 kws. to 186,00 kws., and one station, the

[1] See page 60 ; also page 99 *et seq.*

Lenin Dnieper-hydro electric station, with a power of 310,000 kws.

The following table shows the development of electrification at a glance :

	1913.	1928.	1932.
Capacity (mill. kws.)—			
All plants . . .	1·098	1·874	4·567
Regional stations . .	0·17	0·61	2·624
Output (mill. kw. hours)—			
All plants . . .	1,945·0	5,003·0	13,400·0
Regional stations . .	431·0	1,950·0	7,895·0

The geographical distribution of the electric power industry in the course of the First Piatiletka has been one of the principal factors in the new distribution of the productive forces of the country, assuring as it does both a radical technical reconstruction of the old industrial regions and the creation of a power-supply base for the industrial development of new regions.

The aggregate capacity of the power stations of all the regions comprising the old industrial districts, i.e. the Moscow, Leningrad, Ivanovo regions, and the Gorky territory, has increased from 819,800 kws. to 1,555,100 kws.

In the Urals, in accordance with the Plan, the increase in the capacity of the electric power stations during the First Piatiletka was particularly rapid, rising from 131,100 kws. in 1928 to 434,000 kws. in 1932.

The problem of supplying the Donbas and other industrial districts of the Ukraine with electric power has been solved by an increase in the capacity of the electric power stations in the Ukraine from 465,200 kws. in 1928 to 1,428,900 kws. in 1932.

The capacity of the stations of Transcaucasia has increased from 141,400 kws. to 220,500 kws.

Among the power stations which have been newly erected and radically reconstructed during the Five-Year Plan period, the following occupy an especially prominent place : the Kashira Station, which at the end of the Five-

Year Plan period attained a capacity of 186,000 kws. ; the Shatura Station with 136,000 kws. ; the First Moscow Station (Moges I) with 107,000 kws. ; the Krassny Oktyabr Station with 111,000 kws. ; the Shterovka Station with 157,000 kws. ; the Zuevo Station with 150,000 kws. ; the Gorky Station with 158,000 kws. ; the Chelyabinsk Station with 100,000 kws. ; the Krassnaya Zvezda Station at Baku with 109,000 kws. ; and the greatest hydro-electric station in the world, the Lenin Dnieper Hydro-electric Station, with a capacity at the end of the Five-Year Plan period (when it was set in operation) of 310,000 kws. and with a projected capacity of 558,000 kws.

Machine Construction.

The machine construction industry has given better results than any other ; this is particularly important, because on the one hand the development of the machine construction industry is exactly what the Soviet authorities most desired, and on the other, it, of course, forms the basis for the development of practically every other branch of the national economy.

In accordance with the Five-Year Plan, the output of the machine construction industry in 1932–3 was to have been three and a half times that in 1927–8. Actually, this had already been achieved by 1931, when the value of the output was over six and a half times that in 1913, and in 1932 the Five-Year Plan estimate for the last year (1932–3) was exceeded by over 54 per cent.

Agriculture, and the most important branches of the light and heavy industries, transport, &c., are now being supplied with up-to-date Soviet machines—many of excellent quality.

The output of agricultural machinery during the First Piatiletka increased more than five and a half times. The production of agricultural machinery is concentrated in forty-eight enterprises, the output of which in 1932 was more than sixteen times the output of the 722 small enterprises producing agricultural machinery in pre-revolutionary Russia.

Moreover, from the production of implements for the use of small peasant farming, the industry has passed to the production of implements for the technical re-equipment of agriculture conducted on a larger scale than anywhere else in the world.

During the First Piatiletka a powerful shipbuilding industry has developed. Compared with 1927–8, the output of the Soviet shipyards in 1932 increased 3·5 times.

During the four and a quarter years under review the new, or practically new types of machinery constructed include motor tractors, combines, and all kinds of complex agricultural machinery, motor cars and lorries, aeroplanes, ships, refrigerators, oil tankers, timber haulers, Diesel engines, machinery for the production of armaments, printing machines, pneumatic machines, lathes of all kinds, turbo-generators, equipment for the oil industry, such as cracking plant, boring machinery, &c., machinery for the metallurgical, coal, peat, electrical, and chemical industries, also for the textile and other light industries, &c.

The progress of machine building in the U.S.S.R. during the First Five-Year Plan period was attained firstly as a result of the high rate of development of the old machine-building districts which served as the principal bases for the industrialization of the backward districts, and secondly, by the simultaneous extensive development of machine building in new districts.

In the eastern regions of the U.S.S.R., the following are the most important machine-building plants constructed : the Sverdlovsk Plant for metallurgical equipment, the Chelyabinsk Tractor Plant, the Chelyabinsk Abraisive Plant, the Irkutsk Plant for mining equipment, the Tashkent Plant for agricultural machinery, the Verkhne-Saldinsk Plant for iron constructions, and the iron construction sections at Kuznetskstroy and Magnitostroy. A number of plants have been reconstructed : the Zlatoust Tool-Making Plant, the Ilyich Metal-Working Plant in Tashkent, the Ust-Katava Car-Building Plant, the Chelyabinsk Agricultural Machinery Plant, the Perm Plant for the manufacture of separators, and the Far Eastern works.

Construction is under way on the Komsomol Shipbuilding Wharf in the Far East, on the Tagil Car-Building Plant, the Siberian Textile Equipment Plant, the Sverdlovsk Plant for the production of electrical apparatus, the Carburettor Plant in the Middle Volga region. Construction has also been started on the Kuznetsk Locomotive Building Plant, the Orsk Diesel, and Steam Locomotive Building Plant, the Motor Building Plant in Bashkiria, and others.

This list of the principal machine building units, though it does not by any means exhaust the total program of new construction work which has been accomplished, shows quite clearly that machine building has been distributed more evenly throughout the country—in the Volga regions, the Urals, Western Siberia, and the outlying regions of the national minorities in the U.S.S.R.—thus creating a base for the further industrialization of those regions.

Chemical Industry.

Exclusive of the match, perfumery, and fats industries, fifty-eight large new chemical factories were set into operation during the four and a quarter years of the First Piatiletka. These include works for the manufacture of heavy chemicals, artificial silk, pharmaceutical products, synthetic rubber, artificial dyes, &c.

During the Five-Year Plan period, a number of works for new and most complex branches of heavy chemical industry were built. In the first place, the manufacture of synthetic ammonia, potash, and other mineral salts (chromates, fluorides, &c.) and the production of sulphur, chlorine, insecticides, reagents for flotation processes, &c., was organized.

The heavy chemical industry in pre-revolutionary Russia was built up and developed chiefly on imported raw material and intermediates. During the First Piatiletka a number of most important raw material bases in the Soviet Union were discovered and prepared for development. The rich deposits of apatites, phosphate rock, chromites, barites, sulphur, &c., are now in the service of Soviet industry. The Soviet base of raw material now extends from the North Polar circle to the remotest deserts of Central Asia.

Among other interesting facts it may be mentioned that in 1932 the output of chemical products for general consumption increased 2·4 times, as compared with the output in 1928.

During the First Five-Year Plan period, the aniline dye industry has been completely reconstructed and the production of chemical by-products of the coking industry increased three and a half times. Similarly, the rubber industry has been radically reconstructed and has become a large-scale industry.

The great technical equipment of the rubber industry ensured the completion of its Five-Year Plan in three years. The output of rubber technical goods in 1932 increased 89.3 per cent. as compared with 1913, and 300 per cent. as compared with 1923.

The U.S.S.R. was the first country in the world to have succeeded in producing artificial rubber on an industrial scale, and two factories for its production have already been set into operation.

Light and Food Industries.

The light industries had not fulfilled the Five-Year Plan by the end of 1932, but they have entered on the Second Five-Year Plan with well-equipped factories and with an increased home supply of raw products which assures them more rapid progress within the next few years.

As a result of work under the Five-Year Plan, the output of the light industries in 1932 was 87 per cent. in excess of that in 1928. The goods in circulation in the retail trade was 75 per cent. in excess of 1928. There were 158,000 additional State and co-operative shops as compared with 1929.

During the Piatiletka, thirteen new cotton mills (with 1,000,000 spindles) were set into operation, three stockinette factories, three linen, four woollen, thirteen clothing, four boot and shoe factories, eleven leather works, two cinema film works, &c. &c.

The stockinette, clothing, boot, and leather-making industries have developed from handicraft or very small industrial concerns into huge industries. Many of what might be called the cultural branches of the light industries have also developed rapidly during the four and a quarter years, such as the manufacture of photographic, musical, cinema, and gramophone apparatus, records, &c.

The food industry in four and a quarter years exceeded the schedule of the Five-Year Plan by nearly 9 per cent.

2

The fishing, sugar, and tobacco industries have been completely reorganized and modernized. The meat industry was in the process of being thoroughly reorganized at the end of the Piatiletka.

In the conserving industry in 1928, there were twenty-two primitive factories with a capacity of output of about 100,000,000 tins of conserves annually. But by the end of 1932 there were forty-eight large canning works with a capacity of output of 1,000,000,000 tins of conserves annually.

The development of industrial construction in the East and in the territories of the national minorities of the Soviet Union has not been confined to heavy industry. During the First Five-Year Plan period, the eastern districts have been covered with a dense network of enterprises of the light and food industries. A number of cotton, textile, leather, and shoe factories have been built up in these regions upon their own bases of raw materials and power supply. Many food factories have been established, including sugar plants, canning factories, vegetable oil plants, confectionery works, meat-packing combines, and refrigerating plants.

Among the enterprises of light industry, the following deserve especial mention on account of their importance: a number of newly-built silk mills in the republics of Central Asia and Transcaucasia ; the cotton mills of Fergana and Askhabad ; the large leather factory in the city of Frunze ; two large-scale cotton combines in Tashkent and in Barnaul, still under construction in 1933.

Outstanding among the enterprises of the food industry is the system of canning factories in the principal producing districts of the country, and in such distant regions as Kamchatka ; a number of sugar plants in Kirghizia, Kazakstan, Western Siberia, and the Far East, still in process of construction in 1933 ; and the building of the meat-packing combines in Semipalatinsk, Orsk, and Verkhne-Udinsk.

Agriculture.

Toward the beginning of the First Piatiletka, the characteristic feature of agriculture in the Soviet Union was the overwhelming predominance of small and very small individual peasant holdings.

The average area of cultivation of the individual holdings, which at that time occupied 97·3 per cent. of the total cultivated area, amounted in 1928 to *4·5 hectares* ; and the average area of cultivation of the holdings of poor and middle peasants (exclusive of the sowing area of the kulak holdings) was only *4·03 hectares*.

It was, of course, hopeless to introduce large-scale mechanized farming on these small peasant farms. To do this it was necessary to organize large farms, and this was done on the one hand by the formation of Soviet State farms (sovkhozy), and on the other by encouraging and assisting the formation of collective farms (kolkhozy) by a pooling of the productive resources of the individual peasant farms and by the supply of agricultural machinery, fertilisers, agronomists, &c. to both these forms of large-scale farming.

Special Machine Tractor Stations were organized, which in 1932 numbered 2,446, to supply tractors and other agricultural machinery and skilled scientific assistance to the collective farms.

The plan for collectivization was considerably over-fulfilled by the end of 1932, 61·5 per cent. of the total number of peasant farms having joined collectives. The following table shows the progress made :

	1928.	1932.	Estimate in Five-Year Plan for 1932–33.
Number of collective farms	33,300	211,050	—
Number of former individual farms collectivized . . .	417,700	14,707,700	5,000,000
Sown area (hectares) in kolkhozy . . .	1,370,000	91,579,000	14,500,000
Percentage of total area sown by peasants, cultivated by kolkhozy .	1·2	75·6	20

The total number of State farms increased from 3,125, cultivating 1,735,000 hectares in 1928 to 10,203, cultivating 13,557,000 hectares in 1932.

The following table shows the progress made in the cultivation of some of the most important crops, and in particular by the kolkhozy and sovkhozy :

SOWN AREA IN U.S.S.R.

(IN MILLION HECTARES)

	1913.	1928.			1932.		
			Sown by			Sown by	
	Total Area Sown.	Total Area Sown.	State Farms.	Collective Farms.	Total Area Sown.	State Farms.	Collective Farms.
Total sown area (all crops) . . .	105·50	112·99	1·74	1·37	134·43	13·56	91·58
Under all grain crops .	94·36	92·17	1·10	1·04	99·71	9·30	69·12
Under wheat . .	31·65	27·73	0·35	0·45	34·53	4·51	26·98
Under industrial crops .	4·55	8·62	0·32	0·16	14·88	0·97	11·35
Cotton . . .	0·69	0·97	0·02	0·02	2·17	0·15	1·43
Long fibre flax . .	1·02	1·36	0·01	0·01	2·51	0·05	1·59
Sugar-beet . .	0·65	0·77	0·20	0·01	1·54	0·20	1·11

In 1932 socialized agriculture (State farms and collective farms) supplied 84·2 per cent. of the total marketable grain, 83 per cent. of cotton, and has played a decisive rôle in the course of the Five-Year Plan period in the food supply of the country, in the creation of a raw material base for industry and export.

During recent years the cotton industry received twice as much Soviet-produced cotton as was raised in Russia in 1913. By 1931 the U.S.S.R. had already used considerable quantities of home-grown raw materials in her cotton-textiles industry, and had gone some way towards emancipating herself from cotton imports, which before the war reached 200,000 tons and in 1928 about 144,000 tons.

In addition, a great step forward has been made in the cultivation of the very valuable Egyptian cotton. At the beginning of the Five-Year Plan period hardly a hectare of Egyptian cotton was grown in the U.S.S.R., but in 1932 the area under Egyptian cotton was already 51,000 hectares.

The number of tractors employed in agriculture increased from 26,733, with a total of 278,100 h.p. on October 1, 1928, to (allowing for depreciation) 148,480, with a total 2,225,000 h.p. by January 1, 1933.

The value of agricultural machinery and tractors, which in the beginning of 1928 amounted to 1,099,000,000 roubles, increased by the end of 1932 to 2,380,000,000 roubles. The value of irrigational and ameliorative engineering constructions (not counting the expenditures of the individual collective farmers and individual peasants) rose from 827,000,000 roubles to 1,544,000,000 roubles.

At the beginning of the Five-Year Plan period, the bulk of the machinery made available for agriculture consisted of machines used in raising grain. Toward the end of the First Piatiletka, Soviet industry, in addition to mastering the production of complicated tractor-drawn machinery for the growing of grain, also organized the manufacture of machinery for use in raising technical crops, and in this way established a firm base of modern technical equipment for every branch of agricultural production.

For the purpose of mastering the new technique of mechanized large-scale socialist agriculture, tens of thousands of workers and collective farmers have received and are receiving instruction and training in colleges, universities, and technical schools, while hundreds of thousands and millions have gone and are going through courses in order to raise their skill and qualifications.

In 1932 the number of students in agricultural colleges was 57,700, as compared with 27,300 in 1928. In the agricultural technical schools and secondary vocational schools, 199,800 students received instruction in 1932, as compared with 62,800 in 1928. Finally, the courses of mass training in skilled work were attended in 1932 by 4·5 million persons. To this army of persons fitting themselves for skilled work in agriculture must be added the 53,000 organizers and directors who received their specialized education during this period.

Although there has also been considerable development in the organization of large State and collective stock-breeding farms, the shortage of live stock, brought about as a result of the fierce opposition of the kulak elements to the Soviet policy of the collectivization of agriculture, had not been made good by the end of 1932.

But, in general, it may be said that, in the course of the First Piatiletka, large-scale collective farming became the prevailing and dominant form of agriculture in the Soviet Union, that the U.S.S.R. had become a country of the largest-scale farming in the world, and that collective forms in all branches of agriculture have now undoubtedly come to stay in the U.S.S.R.

Transport.

The development of transport construction proceeded in accordance with those territorial changes which took place in the leading branches of the national economy towards the end of the Five-Year Plan period. Of the 14,000 kms. of new railways started during the Five-Year Plan period, and the 6,500 completed and put in operation toward the end of that period, about 80 per cent. fall to the eastern districts.

The following new lines have been opened : Borovoye-Akmolinsk-Karaganda ;   Leninsk-Novosibirsk, Kartaly-Magnitnaya ;   Kurgan-Sverdlovsk, and others. During the Five-Year Plan, the Turksib railway, with its great length of track, was built, thus establishing a new inter-regional means of communication between Central Asia and Siberia. This trunk-line has created vast possibilities for the development of the productive forces of districts that were formerly isolated from the industrial centres.

Although the Piatiletka for the technical reconstruction and re-equipment of transport had not been completed by the end of 1932, in many other respects transport had exceeded the Five-Year Plan estimates. The transport difficulties experienced have been due, not so much to the failure of the transport system, as to the enormous demands made upon it by the truly tempestuous development of practically all branches of the national economy.

The following table makes clear the achievements of

the railways, and, at the same time, it shows some of the reasons for the difficulties experienced :

	1913.	1928.	1932.	Planned for 1932–3 in Five-Year Plan.
Length of railway lines in operation (in thousand kms.) . .	58·5	76·9	83·3	94·0
Freight carried (in million tons)	132·4	156·2	267·9	480·0
Freight carried (in milliard ton kms.) . .	65·7	93·4	169·3	162·7
Density of goods traffic per km. of railway lines in operation (in thousand ton kms.) .	1,123·0	1,215·0	2,075·0	1,730·0
Number of passengers carried (millions). .	184·8	291·1	967·0	—
Total passengers carried (in milliard passenger kms.). . . .	25·2	24·5	83·7	35·4
Density of traffic per km. of railway lines in operation (in thousand passenger kms.) . .	432·0	320·0	1,008·0	402·0

Great progress was also made in river, marine, and road transport. During the First Five-Year Plan period, several new sea routes have been opened up. Regular traffic has been established over the Kara Sea, and a start has been made in opening up the entire Northern Sea route, from the White Sea to the Behring Straits, for transport.

One of the largest canals in Europe, the White Sea-Baltic Canal, has been built, thus opening the shortest route between Leningrad and the White Sea. A number of river routes have also been opened for navigation, along the whole length of Siberian rivers, the Yenissei, the Ob, the Lena, &c.

Among other facts it may be mentioned that the length

of the navigable riverways in use rose from 71,600 kms. in 1928 to 84,200 kms. in 1932.

During the First Five-Year Plan period 93,000 kms. of new roads were built, of which about 12,000 kms. were coated roads. At the same time the building of roads to open up new regions has assumed considerable importance. The republics of Central Asia, which did not have any regular roads in the past, have been provided with 2,500 kms. of well-metalled roads. Roadmaking has also been started for the first time in the north-eastern parts of the R.S.F.S.R.

At the beginning of the First Piatiletka the country had a total of 18,700 automobiles, practically all of them of foreign make. At the end of the period, as a result of the organization of an automobile industry in the U.S.S.R., the number of motor cars in use reached 75,000, i.e. four times as many as in 1928.

The number of bus lines during the First Five-Year Plan period went up from 265 in 1928 to 582 in 1932, and their length increased from 14,582 kms. in 1928 to 35,255 kms. in 1932.

Civil Aviation.

The beginning of the construction of the civil air fleet in the U.S.S.R. dates back to 1923. On the eve of the First Piatiletka the Soviet civil air lines had a length of 11,442 kms., over which flights totalling 2·8 million kms. had been made and 10,613 passengers, 93·2 tons of mail, and 162·2 tons of freight had been carried. In 1928 air surveys covered an area of 30,700 square kms. and 33,600 hectares were covered from the air in the fight against animal and insect pests in forestry and agriculture. Aerial expeditions covered another 29,900 kms.

As a result of the construction work carried on during the Five-Year Plan period, the length of the air lines in regular use reached 31,934 kms. in 1932, and 31,600 passengers, 430 tons of mail, and 447 tons of freight were carried.

The air lines include such trunk lines as the Moscow-Samara-Orenburg-Tashkent line, the Moscow-Kharkov-Rostov-Mineralnye-Vodi-Baku-Tiflis line, the Moscow-Sverdlovsk-Novosibirsk line, the Irkutsk-Khabarovsk-

Vladivostok line, and the Moscow-Kazan-Magnitogorsk-Karaganda-Alma-Ata line. The area covered by aerial photo surveys in 1932 was four times as large as in 1928.

The plan for aviation work in agriculture and forestry was exceeded many times over. In 1929 an area of 33,500 hectares was covered from the air in the fight against animal and insect pests in forestry and agriculture ; in 1930 the area reached 68,000, hectares ; in 1931, 246,000 hectares ; and in 1932, 1,010,000 hectares. In addition to this, new forms of work were undertaken by agricultural and forestry aviation ; 58,000 hectares were sown by aeroplane and 11·5 million hectares of forest land surveyed during 1932.

During 1932 about 170,000 kms. were covered by aerial expeditions (over 5·5 times as much as in 1928). Heroic work was also done by aviators in the opening up of the Arctic by the Soviet icebreakers (the Kara expeditions, the expeditions to North Land, Novaya Zemlya, Wrangel Island, Taimur Peninsula, &c.).

During the Piatiletka the civil air fleet made notable progress in the work of developing experimental aeroplane and motor construction (the all-metal giant plane ANT—14, the all-steel electrically welded aeroplane Stal—2, the construction of non-rigid airships for training purposes up to 7,800 cubic metres in volume). It has greatly strengthened the technical resources of the air lines and air bases, and created the necessary conditions for an even more extensive development of aviation during the Second Piatiletka.

Condition of Workers.

In the period under review, unemployment has been completely eliminated.

The vast proportion of industrial workers are now on the seven-hour day. In hazardous and underground work and for young workers from sixteen to eighteen years of age, a six-hour work day has been established, and for some groups of workers the work day has been shortened to five or even four hours.

The average number of hours worked per day has been shortened from 9·9 hours in 1913 to 7·8 hours in 1928, and to 7 hours in June 1932, the latter figure including over-time work.

The number of workers in the U.S.S.R. has almost doubled in the course of the First Five-Year Plan, rising from 11·59 million workers and employees engaged in all branches of national economy in 1928 to 22·6 million in 1932, an increase of 96·6 per cent. This growth in the number of workers and employees exceeded the provisions of the Five-Year Plan for the year 1932–3 by 44·5 per cent.

During the Piatiletka the number of women engaged in various branches of national economy more than doubled, and the number of skilled women workers has increased very considerably—in some trades by twenty and more times as much.

The Trade Union membership at the end of 1932 was 17,900,000, or 74 per cent. of the total wage workers in the U.S.S.R.

The average wage has more than doubled in the course of the Five-Year Plan period, exceeding the estimates of the First Piatiletka (for the year 1932–3) by 44 per cent. The movement of wages in various industries has been as follows :

AVERAGE MONTHLY WAGES IN LARGE-SCALE INDUSTRY

	In Roubles.		1932 in Percen-tage Relation to 1928.
	1928.	1932.	
All industry . . .	70·24	116·62	166·0
Coal industry . .	63·27	122·08	193·0
Iron and steel . . .	75·61	132·24	174·9
Engineering machine build-ing (including electric equipment). . .	92·94	142·93	153·8
Chemical . . .	82·09	122·62	149·4
Cotton	59·89	85·89	143·4
Woollen. . . .	63·73	90·16	141·5
Linen . . .	41·58	70·60	169·8
Leather and shoe . .	86·72	112·11	129·3
Food (excluding sugar) .	73·37	101·83	138·8

The annual average wages of agricultural and forestry workers rose from 305·9 roubles in 1928 to 957·9 roubles in 1932, or by 313·2 per cent. ; those of building workers rose from 996·0 roubles in 1928 to 1,509·0 roubles in 1932, and of educational workers from 678 roubles to 1,633 roubles.

The rate of the increase of wages in different branches of industry was determined by the policy of favouring the most important branches and occupations, which accounts for the largest percentage of increase for the coal industry and ferrous metal industry (93·0 per cent. and 74·9 per cent. respectively), and by the endeavour to raise the wages of the previously lowest paid workers.

The greatest rate of increase in wages is shown in agriculture (from 305·9 roubles in 1928 to 957·9 roubles in 1932). The figures for 1928 show the very low wage level of the farm labourers employed by the kulaks, whereas the figures for 1932 apply mainly to the wages of agricultural workers in the State farms and machine and tractor stations.

The wages of educational workers rose 2·4 times, the wage level of these workers having been below the general wage level at the beginning of the Piatiletka.

It should be added that, in addition to monetary wages, the Soviet workers are paid normal wages for all holidays. They have a statutory summer holiday of at least two weeks, and many are enabled to spend their holiday in rest-homes by the sea and in the country free of charge, travelling to and from the rest-home also being free. Rents are graduated in accordance with income, social insurance, comprising sickness benefits, pensions, medical, health treatment at sanatoria, and other benefits is non-contributory—the whole cost being borne by the various enterprises and the State ; the social insurance fund increased from 947,400,000 roubles in 1928 (of which 65,400,000 roubles were for unemployment benefit) to 4,479,300,000 roubles in 1932.

The income of a worker's family has really increased more than the increase in wages indicate, because the average number of wage-earners in a family of an industrial worker in the U.S.S.R. increased from 1·2 at the end of 1928 to 1·5 at the end of 1932.

Along with the considerable rise of the material welfare of the working-class as a whole, there has been a particularly great and rapid rise in the welfare of certain sections of the population whose living standards used to be below the general level : peasants and collective farmers, drawn into industry, have raised their living standards from 2·5 to three times ; families of poor peasants who joined collective farms have increased their income to the level of middle peasants before the latter had joined the collective farms.

During the Five-Year Plan period, there has been a very great reduction of accidents in industry and of sickness among the workers. It is notable that Dr. Frankwood E. Williams, for fifteen years Medical Director of the National Committee of Mental Hygiene in the United States of America, in a recent tour of the U.S.S.R., found that 'a new environment was creating a new kind of human nature, not so subject to many of the troubles he was looking for, such as nervous and mental disease, delinquency, unhappy marriages, or general maladjustment,' and that 'the rate of incidence of nervous and mental disease in Russia is falling.'

This is undoubtedly a result partly of the abolition of unemployment and the fear of unemployment with its attendant worries ; it is also due largely to the improved administration of the public health services.

Health and Housing.

Expenditure for health protection in the U.S.S.R. from all sources (including capital investments) amounted in 1928 to 622,000,000 roubles, and in 1932 to 2,077,500,000 roubles.

On January 1, 1929, the number of hospital beds in the U.S.S.R. was 246,100, and on January 1, 1933, it was 405,800. In the cities the number of hospital beds increased by 58 per cent., and in the rural districts by 90 per cent.

It is interesting to note the considerable increase in the number of medical stations directly serving the workers of large plants and factories. In 1928 there were 1,580 such stations, and in 1932 their number increased to 5,674.

There has been a great increase in the number of crèches. In 1928 there were 43,600 crèches in towns, but in 1932 the number was 286,400 (6·5 times as many). In the agricultural districts the figures were respectively 4,700 and 435,500 (ninety-two times as many).

The sanatorium and health-resort service for workers increased 100 per cent. in the course of the First Piatiletka, 511,000 persons availed themselves of the rest-homes and sanatoria at the expense of the social insurance fund in 1928, while in 1932 the number exceeded 1,000,000 persons.

There has been a notable decline in the mortality of the population of the U.S.S.R. In 1931 the mortality fell 31·5 per cent. as compared with the year 1913, and in the principal proletarian centres the drop was still greater: 40·8 per cent. in Moscow, 41·8 per cent. in Ivanovo, 52·8 per cent. in Yaroslavl, 38·5 per cent. in Perm.

In the course of the Piatiletka, the total capital investments of the socialized sector (state and co-operative) in housing amounted to more than 4 milliard roubles. In addition 400,000,000 roubles were spent on capital renovations of dwellings.

Although there is still a great shortage of dwelling accommodation in the Soviet Union, nevertheless, both in the old and new industrial regions, house building has been developed on a tremendous scale. During the last years the dwelling area in the Donbas region has been doubled, and in the Ural region it increased 2·5 times.

In Moscow over 2,000,000 square metres of floor space were built during the period 1929–32 ; in Leningrad, 1,500,000 square metres; in Kharkov, 503,000 square metres; in Gorky, 456,000 square metres.

The housing conditions of the workers, particularly in the Donbas region, have greatly improved. The workers who had formerly lived in clay huts have moved to new houses. Before the Revolution, in the Ukraine alone, about 40 per cent. of the workers had lived in such huts.

Undoubted successes have been scored by the republics of the national minorities in the matter of improved housing conditions. In the course of four years, investments in house building in Uzbekistan amounted to

48,800,000 roubles ; in the Tadjik Republic, 16,500,000 roubles ; in the Turkoman Republic, 17,800,000 roubles. During these years dozens of new towns and centres grew up in the republics of the non-Russian nationalities.

Education.

The results achieved in the sphere of education are well known and particularly striking. Literacy has been raised from less than 33 per cent. of the population in 1913 to 53·9 per cent. in 1928, and to 90 per cent. in 1932. The number of children in elementary and general secondary schools has increased from less than 8,000,000 in 1913 to 11,600,000 in 1928, and to nearly 22,000,000 in 1932.

As regards higher and technical education, the following table is very striking :

Types of Educational Institutions.	1928.		1932.		1932–3.
	No. of Educational Institutions.	No. of Students.	No. of Educational Institutions.	No. of Students.	No. of Students estimated in the Five-Year Plan.
Academies . .	1	200	23	9,000	—
Higher general educational and technical institutions . .	129	159,800	645	492,300	196,000
Technical colleges	1,650	253,600	3,096	949,200	327,000
Workers' colleges .	147	49,200	1,150	444,400	72,000
Factory schools .	1,814	178,300	3,000	1,177,300	430,000

In 1913 there were only 91 higher educational institutions with 124,000 students, and although much progress had been made in this direction up to 1928, at the beginning of the Five-Year Plan there was still a very great shortage of specialists, and a very few of the latter were of working-class or peasant origin. The Five-Year Plan aimed at altering this state of affairs.

The increase in the number of specialists in all branches of the national economy (not including trade school workers, political educational workers, and part of the trading and administrative staff) is shown in the following table :

| | Number of Specialists. | | | | | |
| Groups of Specialists. | With Higher Education. | | With Secondary Education. | | Total. | |
	End of 1928.	End of 1932.	End of 1928.	End of 1932.	End of 1928.	End of 1932.
In national economy	90,000	184,500	56,000	190,500	146,000	375,000
In education .	26,000	43,200	185,500	344,000	211,500	387,200
Medical cadres .	63,500	76,000	72,000	135,000	135,500	211,000
Total . .	179,500	303,700	313,500	669,500	493,000	973,200

By the end of the First Five-Year Plan period there were about a million persons in the U.S.S.R. with higher and secondary special education. To these should be added about half a million persons with practical experience in industry, in construction, in the transport system, in agriculture, and more than 200,000 in other branches. Thus the Soviet intelligentsia numbered about 1,700,000 persons by the end of the First Five-Year Plan period, and with those engaged in the branches that have not been included in the data of the report, they numbered about 2,700,000.

Of 284,000 new specialists, with higher and secondary education, who completed their course during the Piatiletka, 43·2 per cent. were of working-class origin, and 25·5 per cent. of peasant origin.

The First Five-Year Plan brought about decisive progress in the matter of creating new institutions for the training of specialists in the East, in the Urals, in Siberia, in the Far Eastern territory, and in the republics of the national minorities.

Thus in the republics and regions of the Ural-Kuzbas combine (Ural region, Western Siberian territory, Kazak Autonomous Soviet Socialist Republic, Bashkir Autonomous Soviet Socialist Republic) there were 8,100 students in higher educational institutions at the beginning of the Five-Year Plan period. In Bashkiria and Kazakstan there were no higher educational institutions at all. At the beginning of 1932 the number of students in higher educational institutions in the territory of the Ural-Kuzbas rose to 27,700. In Central Asia the number of students in higher general and technical educational institutions rose to 20,000 as against 3,500 in 1928.

A large number of educational institutions have been opened in the new industrial regions.

A clear indication of the cultural and political advancement of the population is presented by the growth of the Soviet press. In Tsarist Russia, in 1913, the daily newspaper circulation was 2,700,000. At the beginning of the Five-Year Plan period it was 8,800,000 (576 newspapers), and by the end of the First Piatiletka it rose to 36,000,000 (6,500 newspapers).

The number of books (separate titles) published in the first year of the Five-Year Plan period was 34,200 ; at the end of the period the number was 53,800.

It may not be out of place to emphasize here the proportionately more rapid cultural improvements in the areas inhabited by the hitherto subject and most backward nationalities, as a result of the complete reversal in this, as in other respects, of the policy of the Tsarist Government.

Thus expenditure on education per soul of the population has increased as a result of the building of schools, &c. as follows :

	1913–4. Roubles.	1931–2. Roubles.
R.S.F.S.R. as a whole . .	2·83	11·90
Uzbekistan	0·25	28·26
Azerbaijan	0·83	32·60
Turkmenistan . . .	0·50	37·0

In Armenia, where before the Revolution there were no high schools, there were 9 such schools in 1932, with 7,600 students. In Armenian elementary schools in 1919 there were 47,000 pupils. In 1932 there were 216,000 pupils.

In Moldavia, in 1924, there were 11 schools. By 1932 there were 500 schools.

In White Russia, in 1922, there were 1,430 schools,

with 3,000 teachers and 92,000 pupils. In 1932, 7027 schools with 18,000 teachers, and 750,000 pupils.

In the small Republic of Oirat, in Siberia, in 1922, there were 56 schools with 1,500 pupils. In 1932 there were 209 schools with 15,100 pupils. Literacy in Oirat during the same period has increased from 6 per cent. to 94 per cent.

In the Buriat-Mongol Republic in 1921, in the elementary schools, there were 18,000 pupils ; in 1932, 63,000, and 97 per cent. of all children of school age were attending school.

In the Ukraine in 1915, in the elementary schools, there were 1,500,000 pupils. In 1932 the number attending was 4,500,000. Before the war in none of the 17,000 schools in the Ukraine was teaching in the Ukrainian language permitted. In 1932, in 90 per cent. of the total number of schools (21,000) the teaching was in the Ukrainian language, and in other schools the courses were given in the language of the national minorities of the particular district. In 1932 there were 347 Polish schools, 579 German, 495 Jewish schools, &c.

An Academy of Science has been organized in the Ukraine as well as 1,058 scientific institutes with 10,800 scientific workers. There are 78 theatres in the Ukraine, among them 58 where the Ukrainian language is used, 8 Russian, 1 Polish, 1 German, 1 Bulgarian, 1 Gipsy, 1 Greek, and the remaining Jewish.

In White Russia the Soviet Government has founded an Academy of Science, 32 High schools and universities with 15,000 students ; 212 Workers' Clubs, 930 Libraries, 4 Museums, 1,415 Houses of Culture (similar to workers' clubs) 13 theatres, 3 Broadcasting Stations, &c.

Similar progress has been shown by practically every nationality in the U.S.S.R. In a number of cases the native alphabets have been latinized, and in other cases a written language has been created for the first time. The latinized alphabet is now used by 68 nationalities, among them Chinese, Mongols, Buriats, Kalmyks, Turks, Tartars, Bashkirs, Tadjiks, &c. A written language has been created for 42 other nationalities during recent years.

The growth of the press of the national minorities was particularly significant. Books had been published in 36

3

languages in 1913, in 55 languages in 1927–8, and in 90 languages in 1932. In 1928 newspapers were published in 48 languages ; in 1931, in 63 languages. The proportion of books in the languages of the national minorities rose from 18·3 per cent. of the whole quantity of published books in 1928 to 25·2 per cent. in 1931.

The number of reading-rooms in the villages increased from 21,300 to 46,000 ; in addition, 1,500 Houses of Socialist Culture were built. The period of the First Piatiletka was also a period of very considerable growth of the most varied forms of cultural and educational activity, this being an expression of the general cultural advancement of the population of the U.S.S.R.

I I

THE SECOND FIVE-YEAR PLAN

THE SECOND FIVE-YEAR PLAN

THE foundation for the construction of a socialist economy, based on a classless society in the conduct and administration of which all who work by hand and brain are encouraged to take an active part, having been laid in the First Five-Year Plan, the Second Five-Year Plan covering the period 1933–7, sets out to consolidate the achievements of the First Five-Year Plan, to continue the industrialization of the country and to eliminate completely private ownership in the means of production and all capitalist and parasitic elements not only in industry but also in agriculture.

By thus removing the social causes and economic possibility of the exploitation of man by man, it is confidently expected that the capitalist ideology and habits of the past will gradually be erased, and all workers will be transformed ultimately into conscious builders of the new socialist society.

The Plan contains a wide programme for the completion of the technical reconstruction of the national economy on the principles of the most modern technique, and lays special stress on the need for the further training of workers and for the thorough mastery by them of the principles and practice of modern technique. As Stalin said :

> ' The ardour of new construction must be supplemented in the Second Five-Year Plan by the ardour of the mastery of new plants and new technique, by a serious rise in labour productivity and a serious lowering in production costs.'

The Plan aims further at promoting co-operation between the town and country, thus consolidating the economic and political foundations of the Soviet system and the union of the town workers and peasants for the organization of a classless socialist society.

It is hoped in the course of the Second Five-Year Plan to make a considerable step forward in eliminating the contrast between life in the town and village. On the one hand, agriculture is to be industrialized, and farm labour being largely mechanized will become a variety of industrial labour. On the other, the amenities of the town are to be introduced as rapidly as possible into the village. Transport connexions between the towns and villages will be greatly developed ; at the same time, the towns are to be supplied with more and more open spaces, gardens, sports grounds, &c.

Other important aims of the plan are to strengthen the defensive capacity of the Soviet Union and to transform her into one of the most technically advanced countries in the world, and to make her economically and technically independent.

The Plan also provides for a considerable increase in the standard of life and the educational and cultural level of all the nationalities inhabiting the U.S.S.R., and for this purpose it is proposed to speed up the output of the industries producing the means of consumption at a greater rate than during the First Piatiletka, and than that of the industries producing the means of production.

Among the organizational methods proposed to ensure the fulfilment of the Second Five-Year Plan are the following :

The elimination of bureaucracy from economic administration, and the insistence on personal responsibility for managerial and other work entrusted to particular persons.

The concentration of the best engineering-technical forces in the most important production sectors, rather than in offices.

The allocation of wages in accordance with the quality and quantity of work put in, thus providing a material stimulus for the individual worker to raise his labour productivity.

Stimulation of socialist competition, particularly with a view to encouraging the mastery of new technique and new lines of production.

Firm production discipline both in industrial establishments and State farms, as well as in collective farms.

Revolutionary vigilance against the remaining enemies of the Soviet State.

NEW CONSTRUCTIONS

The completion of the technical reconstruction of the national economy and the planned dimensions of the production programme in industry, agriculture and transport necessitate the fulfilment of a vast programme of new constructions during the Second Five-Year Plan. To meet this programme, it is proposed to invest for capital construction work during the Second Five-Year Plan a total of 133,400,000,000 roubles (in 1933 prices) in the national economy of the U.S.S.R., i.e. 2·6 times the sum so invested during the period of the First Five-Year Plan.

Of this sum 69,500,000,000 roubles are to be invested in industry as against 25,000,000,000 roubles so invested in the period of the First Piatiletka ; 15,200,000,000 roubles are to be invested in agriculture as against 9·7 milliard roubles during the First Five-Year Plan and 26,500,000,000 roubles in transport as against 8·9 milliard roubles during the first Piatiletka. Of the 69·5 milliard roubles to be invested in industry, 53·4 milliards are to be invested in the heavy industries as against 21·3 milliards invested in the First Five-Year Plan (an increase of 2·5 times) and 16·1 milliards in the light industries as against 3·5 milliards in the First Five-Year Plan (i.e. an increase of 4·6 times).

It is calculated that during the Second Piatiletka the total basic capital of the Soviet national economy will increase from 85 milliard roubles at the end of 1932 to 195 milliard roubles in 1937 (in 1933 prices), which represents a growth in basic capital of 2·3 times. This includes industry from 25·5 milliard roubles at the end of 1932 to 77·0 milliard roubles in 1937 ; agriculture from 11·4 milliard roubles to 22·6 milliard roubles, and transport from 19·8 milliard roubles to 38·5 milliard roubles.

Productive capacity in the most important branches of industry is to increase as follows : pig-iron, 2·3 times ; the coal industry, more than double ; generator construction, 2·4 times ; the automobile industry, almost four times ; locomotive construction, more than treble ; railroad car building, 3·9 times ; district electric stations, 2·5 times ; the footwear industry, double ; the cotton industry, 1·5 times ; the linen industry, more than double ;

the sugar industry, 1·5 times ; the large meat combinats, 2·5 times, &c.

Special attention is to be paid to the following new constructions :

Machine Building.

The completion of the construction begun during the First Five-Year Plan of the Urals Heavy Machine Building Plant with 100,000 tons capacity ; of the Kramatorsk Plant with 150,000 tons capacity ; of the Chemical Apparatus Plant in the Urals ; of the Lugansk Locomotive Plant with an annual capacity of 1,080 locomotives, ' FD ' type ; of the Orsk Locomotive and Diesel Engine Plant producing 500 locomotives and 500 Diesels annually ; of the Kashira Electric Locomotive Plant designed to produce 300 main-line electric locomotives ; of the Urals Carriage Building Plant with an output of 54,000 four-axle cars ; the Kuznetsk and Irkutsk Carriage Constructing Plants with a capacity of 10,000 four-axle carriages each ; of the Motor Plant in Ufa to produce 50,000 motors ; of the Kharkov Turbo-Generator Station with a capacity of 1·5 million kws. ; to increase the output of the Gorki Automobile Plant to 300,000 automobiles ; of the Stalin (AMO) Auto Plant to 80,000 cars ; of the Yaroslavl Plant to 25,000 five-ton trucks, as well as others.

The construction during the Second Five-Year Plan of the Ufa and Stalingrad Auto Plants with a productive capacity of 100,000 three-ton trucks each ; of the Samara Auto Plant with an output of 25,000 five-ton trucks ; of plants producing polishing, boring, gear-shaping, automatic, and heavy lathes ; of a new powerful ball-bearing plant with an output of 24 million ball bearings ; of a plant in the Urals to produce electrical apparatus and transformers ; the construction of a group of plants producing textile machines and equipment for the food industry and so on.

Iron and Steel Industry and Non-Ferrous Metallurgy.

The completion of the construction of the Magnitogorsk Plant with a productive capacity of 2·7 million tons of cast iron; of the Zaporozhie, Nizhni-Tagil, Azov Steel, Krivoi Rog, Lipetsk, Tula, and other metallurgical plants; the development of the construction and putting into operation of the first units of the Baikal, Khalilov, second Kuznetsk and Far East plants, of pipe-casting plants, and others.

In non-ferrous metallurgy the following plants are to be completed: the Pribalkhash Copper Combinat with a capacity of 100,000 tons; the Middle Urals Combinat of 50,000 tons capacity; the Kazakstan Polymetallic Combinat with a capacity of 60,000 tons of lead; zinc plants in the cities of Chelyabinsk and Ordzhonikidze, the Altai Poly-metallic Combinat, Kemerovo, and so on; completion of the Volkhov and Dnieper Aluminium Plants; the construction of a new aluminium plant in the Urals with a capacity of 25,000 tons and of an aluminium plant in Karelia with a capacity of 8,000 tons; the construction of magnesium, nickel, and other non-ferrous plants.

Coal.

The development of the construction of new large mines and the putting into operation of 178 mines with a pro-ductive capacity of 143 million tons of coal annually.

Oil.

The construction of a new group of oil refineries (46 pipe-still units for primary distillation and 93 cracking units). The construction of pipe-lines for the transport of petroleum and petroleum products over a total length exceeding 4,000 kms. Construction of enterprises for the peat and shale industries is also to be developed.

Chemistry.

The construction of new fertilizer combinats, synthetic rubber plants, soda plants, sulphuric acid, rubber com-position materials, dye and paint plants, rayon factories, and so on.

Electrification.

The construction of 79 district stations, which is to include the completion of the construction of the Zuevo

Station with a capacity of 250,000 kws.; of the Gorki Station of 204,000 kws.; of the Shatura Station with a capacity of 180,000 kws.; of the Dubrovka Station of 100,000 kws.; of the Svir No. 3 Power Station of 96,000 kws. capacity; the completion of the Dnieper Hydro-electrical Station with a capacity of 558,000 kws.

The construction of several new large central stations—in Stalinogorsk with a capacity of 400,000 kws.; in Kemerovo with a capacity of 148,000 kws., also new large stations in the Donbas; of the Chirchik No. 1 Hydro-electrical Station with a capacity of 170,000 kws.; of the Kanakirsk Station of 88,000 kws.; of a station on the river Khram of 60,000 kws. capacity; of No. 2 Station on the Svir of 144,000 kws. capacity; of the Tuloma, and other stations. There is also to be an intensive development in the construction of the stations of Srednevolgastroi (Central Volga Construction)—of the Yaroslavl Station with 100,000 kws. capacity; of the Perm Station of 310,000 kws. capacity, and of the Gorki Station of 200,000 kws. capacity.

Work is to proceed with the construction of several large heating and power stations for the central heating of towns, such as the Moscow-Narvsk and Okhta Stations in Leningrad; the Stalin and Frunze Stations in Moscow; the Sormovo-Kanavinsk Station; the Krasnozavodsk Station in Kharkov, &c.; also of several large district power stations serving factories and plants — one in Magnitogorsk with a capacity of 198,000 kws., another in Kuznetsk with a capacity of 108,000 kws., and others.

Light Industry.

In the light industry there are to be constructed 15 big cotton textile mills, including the Tashkent, Barnaul, Khojent, Charjui, and Transcaucasia Cotton Combinats with a capacity of 200,000 spindles each; 12 large woollen factories with a capacity of output of from 8 to 15 million metres of cloth each per annum; 12 linen mills with a capacity of from 18,000 to 27,000 spindles each; 18 big knitting factories; 11 silk factories; 21 footwear factories with a capacity of output of 100 million pairs.

Food Industry.

In the food industry there are to be completed 17 meat-packing plants begun in the First Five-Year Plan, whilst the construction of 23 new combinats are to be started. A large number of sugar refineries and six soap factories are also to be constructed. There is to be a great increase of the fishing fleet, as well as the construction of canneries, vegetable oil pressing, and confectionery plants, and so on.

Timber Industry.

In the timber industry a large number of saw mills, wood, chemical, and other plants are to be built, and it is hoped to complete the Kama and Kondopoga Cellulose-Paper Combinats, of the Syas Cellulose Combinat, as well as the construction of the Bashkir and Krasnoyarsk Paper Combinats, &c.

There is to be an extensive construction and reconstruction of thousands of local industrial plants producing consumers' goods, about 2 milliard roubles being invested in these enterprises during the Second Piatiletka.

Municipal Construction.

In municipal construction the programme of work includes : extensive improvement work in hundreds of industrial centres ; construction of thousands of dwellings with apartments equipped with all conveniences, aggregating 64 million square metres of floor space ; developing of the work of planning and improving town transport, water supply, sewage, street pavement, planting of trees, and laying out of gardens, and so on ; the building of Houses of Soviets, Houses of Technique, parks of culture and rest, stadia, theatres, clubs, cinemas ; the construction in Moscow of a Palace of Soviets and the first underground railway in the U.S.S.R., the first section of which is to enter into operation in 1934.

REDISTRIBUTION OF PRODUCTIVE FORCES : DEVELOPING NEW REGIONS

We have seen in the summary of the First Piatiletka how a successful beginning was made to bring industry nearer the sources of the raw materials of the U.S.S.R. by developing new areas ; thus, amongst other important things, putting an end to the economic and cultural backwardness of the various national Republics and areas of the U.S.S.R. and relieving the transport system of a considerable amount of work. This work is to be pushed forward during the Second Five-Year Plan.

The proposed programme of extensive new construction involves determined changes in the distribution of the productive forces. Side by side with the development of the old industrial centres, new citadels of industry are being created in the Eastern parts of the Union (Urals, Western and Eastern Siberia, Bashkiria, Far Eastern region, Kazakstan, and Central Asia). The machine construction, metal, coal, oil, electric power, and other industries are being developed intensively in these districts. About half the investments on new constructions in heavy industry will go to the Eastern regions.

In 1937 the Eastern districts will produce one-third of the total iron output of the U.S.S.R., as against a fourth in 1932, about a fifth of the total electric energy (generated by regional stations) as compared with 6·5 per cent. in 1932, and a tenth of the machine construction output as against 5 per cent. in 1932.

It is further proposed to complete the second coal and metallurgical base of the Union, namely, the Ural-Kuznetsk Combinat, which will receive about a fourth of the total capital investments in the national economy of the U.S.S.R., and over a third of the investments in heavy industry. The Ural-Kuznetsk Combinat is scheduled to produce in 1937 one-third of the iron and steel, over one-fourth of the coal, one-sixth of the electric energy of the regional power stations, and about 10 per cent. of the machinery produced in the Soviet Union.

Similarly the geographical distribution of the light and food industries is also being changed. Thus, out of the fifteen cotton textile combinats to be built during the

Second Five-Year Plan, ten will be built in Central Asia, Siberia, and Transcaucasia, involving an increase in the production of cotton textiles in Central Asia of nearly sixteen times as compared with twice in the U.S.S.R. as a whole, and the creation of a firm textile base in these hitherto backward regions.

In the linen industry powerful processing plants are being established in the Western District, the Gorki Area, and in White Russia. New raw material bases are being created and new sugar refineries are being built in Western Siberia, Kirghizia, the Far Eastern region, Transcaucasia, and so on.

Leather, woollen, vegetable oil, and other factories of the light and food industries are being built in the basic centres producing agricultural raw products. The output of local fuels is growing on a large scale, thereby lessening the dependence of a number of districts on outside coal.

Extensive industrial construction is to be developed in regions which were formerly backward industrially, such as Central Volga, the Tartar Republic, North Caucasus, Central Black Earth Province, Transcaucasia, Karelia, Murmansk Province, Far East, Eastern Siberia, and so on ; there is also to be an intensive development of education, health protection, and the press in the national republics and regions.

At the same time there is to be a further development of the old industrial regions of the U.S.S.R., and the process of specialization and of bringing about a more even distribution of industry within particular regions begun in the First Five-Year Plan is to be continued.

Agriculture.

In the field of agriculture there is to be a considerable increase of grain production in the basic grain-growing regions ; the commencement of extensive irrigation work in the Volga district, and the creation of a stable wheat belt in the central and northern regions, a tremendous increase of the output of industrial crops in the principal regions of their production, coupled with the creation of a new sugar-beet base in the East, and an extensive development of new highly valuable crops, particularly in the sub-tropical regions.

Transport.

Side by side with the reconstruction and strengthening of the main trunk lines in an eastern and southern direction, the Plan provides for the building of a large group of new railways and waterways, to link up the new industrial centres with the general transport system of the Union and to serve as a basis for the industrial development of the newly developing regions (Karaganda-Balkash, Ufa-Sterlitamak, Rubtsovka-Ridder, Tomsk-Chulym, the Baltic-White Sea Canal, and so on).

As in the First, so in the Second Piatiletka, detailed figures of development and output have been fixed for all branches and sections of the national economy. Of these we now propose to give a brief summary.

INDUSTRY

In 1937, i.e. the last year of the Second Five-Year Plan, the value of the total output of industry in 1926–7 prices is to reach 92,700,000,000 roubles, as compared with 43,300,000,000 roubles in 1932 (the last year of the First Five-Year Plan completed in four and a quarter years), i.e. an increase of 2·1 times and about six times that of the output of pre-war industry in Russia.

The average annual increase in the output of industry as a whole is fixed at 16·5 per cent.; the average annual rate of increase in the output of articles of consumption to be 18·5 per cent. (as against 17 per cent. in the First Five-Year Plan), whilst that of the means of production is to be 14·5 per cent. Stress is thus laid on the more rapid increase in the rate of production of the means of consumption.

The output of the principal industries in 1937 is estimated as follows. The first column gives the output in 1932:

Industry.	Output in 1932.	1937 Plan of Production.	Percentage of 1932.
All Industry (in milliard roubles) [1] .	43·3	92·7	214·1
Output of means of production . .	23·1	45·5	197·2
Output of articles of consumption .	20·2	47·2	233·6
People's Commissariat of Heavy Industry (in milliard roubles) . .	14·3	33·5	234·6
People's Commissariat of Timber and Forestry (in milliard roubles) .	1·8	3·6	200·0
People's Commissariat of Light Industry (in milliard roubles) . .	7·8	19·5	248·8
People's Commissariat of Supplies (in milliard roubles)	4·6	11·9	256·1
Machine construction and metal working (in milliard roubles) . .	9·2	19·5	207·0
Including :			
Metal cutting lathes (number in thousands)	15·0	40·0	267·0
Tractors calculated as 15 h.p. each (number in thousands) .	50·6	167·0	323·0
Combines (number in thousands) .	10·0	20·0	200·0
Main line locomotives (calculated as Types ' E ' and 'SU ' in units) .	828	2,800	337
Two-axle freight cars (number in thousands)	22·3	118·4	531
Automobiles (number in thousands)	23·9	200	837·0
Electric power (in milliard kw. hours) .	13·4	38	283·0
Including :			
District stations	8·3	24·5	296
Coal (in million tons) . . .	64·3	152·5	237
Crude oil and gas (in million tons) .	22·3	46·8	210
Pig-iron (in million tons) . . .	6·2	16	260
Steel (in million tons) . . .	5·9	17	289
Rolled metal (in million tons) . .	4·3	13	303
Chemical industry (in milliard roubles)	1·9	5·5	280
Lumber (sawn in million cubic metres)	24·5	43	176
Cotton materials (in million square metres)	2,720	5,100	188
Linen materials (in million square metres)	130	600·0	461
Boots and shoes (in million pairs) .	81·9	180	220
Granulated sugar (in thousand tons) .	828	2,500	302
Haul of fish (in thousand tons) . .	1,300	1,800	139
Meat (People's Commissariat of Supplies, in million tons) . .	435	1,200	276
Preserves (in millions of cans) . .	600	2,000	335

During the course of the Second Piatiletka there is to be a rise in the productivity of labour in industry by 63 per cent. as against 41 per cent. in the First Five-Year Plan. At the same time, there is to be a fall in the cost of production by about 26 per cent., whilst a marked improvement in the quality and assortment of output in all branches of

[1] The values in the above table are given throughout in 1926–7 prices.

the national economy is to be secured simultaneously with the fall in production costs.

It is important to note further that, whereas during the Second Piatiletka the amount invested in capital constructions in industry is estimated to be about 2·6 times the amount so invested during the First Piatiletka, the value of the enterprises to be brought into operation during the Second Piatiletka is calculated to amount to 4·4 times that during the First Piatiletka. This is due largely to the increase in the number of skilled workers and experts, and to the work of new enterprises already in operation ; all this has made it possible for new constructions to be carried out at a lower cost, and to complete them in far shorter periods than was the case during the First Piatiletka.

In the course of the Second Five-Year Plan it is proposed to carry out the technical re-equipment of all branches of the national economy of the U.S.S.R., so as to ensure the introduction as rapidly as possible of the latest technical achievements. By 1937 nearly 80 per cent. of the entire output of industry should come from enterprises built or entirely reconstructed during the First and Second Piatiletkas.

The means of production added to the national economy during the years of the Second Piatiletka alone should amount by the end of 1937 to about 50 per cent. to 60 per cent. of the total means of production then in operation.

It is further hoped to complete, in the main, the mechanization of all heavy processes in industry. The Plan provides for the creation of a new energy base for the completion of the reconstruction of all branches of the national economy and for the formation of power reserves at all energy junctions, thus ensuring an uninterrupted supply of electricity for the national economy.

It is also proposed to complete, in the main, the electrification of industry by the widest utilization of the latest electrical methods of production in all branches of industry, especially in metallurgy and chemistry (the consumption of energy by electrically-run industries is to increase more than nine times), by a wide development of the electrificacation of transport and the gradual introduction of electric energy in the productive processes of agriculture.

The Plan further provides for the central heating of

industry in the large cities and for the continuation of the policy of the wider utilization of local fuel in electric power stations—coal from the Moscow Basin, Urals, East Siberia, Central Asia ; the use of peat and shale—and especially water-power resources.

It is sought to complete in the Second Five-Year Plan the linking of district stations within the limits of the districts and to begin the inter-district linking of stations. In the course of the Second Piatiletka the largest system of electric supply in the world (Donbas-Dnieper area), with an output of 9 milliard kilowatt hours per annum is to be established. The gasification of peat and shale is also to be developed.

MACHINE CONSTRUCTION

In the course of the Second Piatiletka, the machine construction industry is to undergo such a reconstruction and development as would enable it to provide all the needs of the Soviet national economy for the most advanced modern technical equipment. The highest rate of development is estimated to take place in the motor tractor industry and in the production of transport and textile machinery.

It may be mentioned in particular that the output of motor cars and lorries during the Second Piatiletka is to increase more than eight times ; that of goods trucks over five times ; main-line locomotives, nearly 3·4 times ; textile equipment for specialized textile work, about six times ; the machine tool industry is to increase its output about three times, &c.

Out of the total output of the machine construction and metal working industry, about one-half will go to supply the need of capital constructions which is estimated to require 9,600,000,000 roubles' worth of equipment in 1937, as against 3,320,000,000 roubles' worth which it received in 1932.

The value of the machinery supplied for capital construction in the heavy industries alone will increase from 1,300,000,000 roubles in 1932 (including imports) to 2,330,000,000 roubles in 1937. But in spite of the great increase of output, it is expected that during the first years of the Second Piatiletka (and until the technique of this

4

branch of production has been fully mastered) the position with regard to the supply of equipment for the heavy industries, particularly for the machine construction and chemical industries and for the construction of prime movers (internal combustion engines), rolling mills, &c., will be considerably strained.

It is estimated that, in the course of the Second Five-Year Plan, about 200 new types and dimensions of lathes will be produced as well as a large variety of machine tools.

The production of metallurgical equipment will be concentrated mainly in the new Urals and Kramatorsk Plants. During the Second Piatiletka some 300,000,000 roubles will be spent for capital constructions in each of these works, and in 1937, when they are expected to work to about 70 per cent. to 78 per cent. of their final capacity, it is estimated that their total output will be about 2·5 times that in 1932.

The output of the principal items of equipment for power production is estimated as follows :

	During the whole Five Years.	1937.	1937 as percentage of 1932.
Steam boilers (thousand square metres)	1,410	385	962·5
Turbines (thousand kws.) .	5,265	1,400	619·5
Prime movers (internal combustion) (thousand kws.) .	6,213	2,600	1,427·8
Generators (thousand kws.) .	5,655	1,400	144·9

The Plan also provides for extending and initiating the construction of various new types of equipment for the production of electrical power, such as new types of turbo-generators of 50,000 kws.; generators of 100,000 kws. aggregate ; powerful transformers with 110,000 to 220,000 volts ; synchronous compensators up to 25,000 to 50,000 kws., &c.

The production of electro-technical equipment is to be developed for bloomings, rolling mills, for various processes in mining, for the metallurgical, for the non-terrous metals and chemical industries, electrical welding, &c.

It is estimated that the output of various machinery for the oil industry and for peat raising will be trebled as compared with 1932.

The mechanization of the timber industry is also to be extended, and the value of the equipment to be supplied to it in 1937 will total some 180,000,000 roubles as compared with 35,000,000 roubles in 1932.

New equipment for the light and food industries will include dozens of new types of machinery. The value of the output of the specialized textile machine construction works alone is estimated to increase from 60,000,000 roubles in 1932 to 360,000,000 roubles in 1937.

The value of the output of the specialized works for the production of machinery for the food industry is estimated to increase from 47,700,000 roubles in 1932 to 140,000,000 roubles in 1937. It should be noted that a considerable quantity of equipment for the light and food industries are also to be manufactured in machine construction works other than the specialized works mentioned above.

The agricultural machinery produced is to include all forms of machinery and tractors for transport necessary to effect a further mechanization of agriculture, and especially the mechanization of processes employed in raising technical and other crops requiring a great deal of labour. Already during the first Piatiletka it is claimed that an agricultural machine construction industry second to none in the world had been created, and the Second Piatiletka seeks nearly to treble the supply of all forms of agricultural machinery, including combines, tractors, &c., for Soviet agriculture. The value of this equipment will increase from 715,000,000 roubles' worth in 1932 to 1,950,000,000 roubles in 1937.

The tractors produced during the Second Piatiletka are to have a total power treble that of the total tractor park at the end of 1932, and the total power of the tractors manufactured in 1937 alone will exceed the power of the total tractor park at the beginning of 1933.

It is estimated that tractor output in 1937 will be as follows: the Kharkov Tractor Works constructing 15 h.p. tractors, 36,000 tractors (apart from spare parts); the Chelyabinsk Works constructing caterpillar tractors of 48 h.p., 20,000 tractors, together with a corresponding quantity of spare parts ; the Stalingrad Factory, reconstructed to produce caterpillar tractors, will have an output of 30,000 tractors. In addition, 10,000 special tractors are also to be manufactured in 1937 at the Krassny Putilovetz Works.

The average power of Soviet tractors in 1937 is estimated to be 41·5 h.p. as against only 26 h.p. in the U.S.A. Also, whereas in the U.S.A., eighty different types of tractors are being manufactured, in the U.S.S.R. there will only be four types.

The tractor industry in the U.S.S.R. will be more concentrated than in the U.S.A. In the latter, in 1929, twelve works produced 229,600 tractors ; in the U.S.S.R. in 1937, 96,000 tractors will be produced in only four works.

The following other items of estimated output of the machine construction industry may be enumerated :

The value of the output of equipment for railway transport will increase from 320,000,000 roubles in 1932 to about 1,580,000,000 roubles in 1937.

Shipbuilding is to increase its output by 2·5 times by the end of the Second Piatiletka ; more complex and modern vessels for marine and river traffic are to be produced, and wharves and shipbuilding yards are to be provided with up-to-date equipment.

The output of equipment for postal, telegraph, telephone, and radio requirements will increase from 285,000,000 roubles in 1932 to 800,000,000 roubles in 1937.

The machine construction plan also provides for great increases in the output of industrial safety appliances ; for equipment for the needs of housing, road building, and municipal construction (buses, trams, taxis, central-heating appliances, &c.) ; equipment for the automatic regulation of various technological processes for aviation, meteorology, calculating machines, &c.

During the last few years there has been a shortage of metal goods required for industrial and construction purposes (bolts, nails, wires, &c.), the Second Piatiletka provides for putting an end to such a shortage by trebling the output of such goods.

The output of consumer's metal goods, including bicycles, radio receiving sets, cameras, &c., in the enterprises of the Commissariat for Heavy Industries in 1937 is to increase 4·2 times as compared with 1932.

The production of all sorts of new types of machinery and equipment is being introduced in Soviet works in the course of the Second Piatiletka.

It is estimated that *in 1937 about 90 per cent. of the output in the All-Union enterprises of the Commissariat for Heavy Industries will be produced in new or completely reconstructed works*, and special care and attention is being devoted to the mastery of the new technological processes and to the rational exploitation of the new machinery and equipment. The plan fixes a reduction of 40 per cent. in the cost of production in the machine construction !ustry, and an increase in the productivity of labour of ðJ per cent.

It is estimated that during the Second Piatiletka 7,910,000,000 roubles will be invested for new capital constructions in the machine building industry made up as follows :

	Sum to be invested during Second Piatiletka.	Percentage of total sum to be invested in Second Piatiletka.	Percentage of total sum invested in First Piatiletka.
New constructions .	5,480 million roubles	69·3	45·3
Extension and reconstruction . .	1,400 ,, ,,	17·7	46·0
Capital repairs . .	580 ,, ,,	7·3	5·0
Other expenditure .	450 ,, ,,	5·7	3·7
	7,910 ,, ,,	100·0	100·0

The smaller proportion invested in extensions and reconstructions is due to the fact that the possibility of such work on existing enterprises is drawing to a conclusion.

ELECTRIFICATION

During the Second Piatiletka, an effort is to be made to electrify completely most branches of industry. The total consumption of electrical energy by the Soviet industries is to increase from 8·7 milliard kw. hours in 1932 to 27 milliard kw. hours in 1937. During the five years the electrical energy supplied to the metallurgical, chemical, and machine construction industry is to increase nine times as compared with 1932, whilst the consumption of electricity in railway transport will increase from 300,000,000 kw. hours in 1932 to 1·6 milliard kw. hours in 1937. (The electrification of the railways is dealt with in the chapter on Transport.)

Electricity is to be introduced wherever possible in agriculture, and it is estimated that by 1937 the consumption of electrical energy in productive processes of agriculture will be ten to fifteen times as much as that consumed in 1932.

Tremendous increases in the consumption of electricity in the homes of the people, for street lighting, and other municipal purposes are also envisaged, the total requirements for electrical energy of the whole national economy of the U.S.S.R. by 1937 being estimated at 38 milliard kw. hours as compared with 13·4 milliard kw. hours consumed in 1932.

The plan of output of electrical energy in the Second Piatiletka is based on the organization of powerful electrical stations (using as far as possible local fuel supplies) in all regions of the U.S.S.R., the output of which will be sufficient to cover, and if necessary more than cover, the above-estimated requirements.

The experience accumulated in the course of the First Five-Year Plan period in the building of huge hydro-electric stations made it possible to start at the beginning of the Second Five-Year Plan period still greater works in connexion with the building of hydro-electric stations on the Middle Volga (Gorky, Yaroslavl), and on the Kama (Perm).

The concentration of the supply of electricity from large district stations started in the First Piatiletka is to be carried very much further during the Second Piatiletka.

Thus, at the beginning of the First Piatiletka in 1928, there were no stations with a capacity of 100,000 kws. and over ; by 1932 there were ten such stations with a combined capacity of 1,409,500 kws. producing 4,200,000,000 kw. hours annually, but in 1937 there are to be twenty-eight such stations with a combined capacity of 4,459,500 kws., producing 18,000,000,000 kw. hours annually, or 47 per cent. of the total output of electricity in that year over the whole of the U.S.S.R.

The building of these powerful stations will be accompanied by the further use of more powerful and modern installations. Thus, in 1932, the total capacity of stations using turbo-generators of 22,000 kws. and over was 1,598,600 kws. (34 per cent. of the total capacity), but it is estimated that in 1937 the total capacity of stations using turbo-generators of 22,000 kws. and over will be 5,888,600 kws., i.e. 55 per cent. of the total capacity of the electric stations of the U.S.S.R. All new stations are now installed with generators of 25,000 to 50,000 kws., and towards the end of the Piatiletka one or two turbo-generators of 100,000 kws. are to be installed.

The linking up of the huge electrical stations and the supply of electricity over wide areas along high voltage transmission lines, started in the First Piatiletka, is being extensively developed during the Second Piatiletka, particularly in the important industrial areas, such as Moscow, Leningrad, the Southern Coal Metallurgical Base, and the Urals-Kuznetsk Combine, thus making possible the electrification of their industries as well as providing electricity for the household needs of these areas.

Among the systems to be further linked up by high voltage transmission lines are the Moscow-Ivanovo-Gorki electrical stations ; the Northern and Southern Urals with the Central Urals ; the Donetz Basin with the Dnieper Power Station—the linking up of the latter will result in an electrical transmission system with an annual output of over 9,000,000,000 kw. hours—the longest system of its kind in the world.

By the end of 1932 the total length of high voltage transmission lines was 9,820 kms., the voltage being 22,000 to 160,000 volts. In 1937 the length of high voltage lines will be 26,250 kms., of which 1,200 kms. will have a voltage of 220,000 volts—the latter are the lines Bobrik-Moscow ; Svir-Leningrad and the line joining the Northern with the Southern Urals.

The investments for the principal new constructions and reconstructions in connexion with district electrical stations during the Second Piatiletka will total about 5,350,000,000 roubles as against 1,900,000,000 roubles so invested in the First Piatiletka.   Of this sum, 3,600,000,000 roubles will be spent on the construction of power stations. In addition, considerable investments are to be made for starting hydro-electrical stations and central systems scheduled to be set into operation in the course of the Third Five-Year Plan.

The programme of construction in connexion with electrification was given briefly under the chapter ' New Constructions.' For the electrification of agriculture, see chapter on Agriculture.

FUEL

In accordance with the plan of development of the national economy generally, the Second Piatiletka estimates the industrial requirements in 1937 at 180,000,000 tons of conventional fuel,[1] i.e. 95·5 per cent. in excess of that consumed in 1932.   In order to satisfy this demand as well as the demand of other consumers and the building up of the necessary reserves, the plan fixes the total output in 1937 at a minimum of 195,000,000 tons of conventional fuel, i.e. 102·0 per cent. in excess of that consumed in 1932.

The consumption of fuel for coking, gas manufacture, &c., in 1937 is estimated to be 154·9 per cent. in excess of that used in 1932 : that consumed in electrical stations, 142·8 per cent. in excess ; on the railways, 58·8 per cent. in excess, and that consumed by the urban population, 94·8 per cent. in excess of 1932.

To assure a constant and adequate supply of fuel not only is the output of the various fuels being increased, but the utilization of fuel is being rationalized, by-products useful as fuels are being more and more utilized, and considerable additional energy is being obtained by the use of water power wherever practical.

Coal.

The output of coal is to increase at a greater rate than other fuels.   In 1937 it is to constitute 68·2 per cent. of

---

[1] One metric ton of conventional fuel represents 7,000,000 large calories.

the total fuel supply as against 60·8 per cent. in 1932. The output of coal and the comparatively higher rates of development of the hitherto secondary regions and also of the new regions can be seen from the following table :

	1932. Tons.	1937. Tons.
Donetz	43,818,000	80,000,000
Moscow	2,850,000	10,000,000
Urals	3,106,000	13,000,000
Kuzbas.	7,040,000	20,000,000
Eastern Siberia . . .	2,182,000	4,500,000
Central Asia	720,000	3,000,000
Far East	1,892,000	6,500,000
Karaganda	722,000	7,000,000
Total .	62,330,000	144,000,000
New coal regions (including Spitzbergen, Pechora, &c.) .	530,000	6,000,000
Industrial co-operative coal mines	1,450,000	2,500,000
Grand total .	64,310,000	152,500,000

The total output capacity of the mines of the U.S.S.R. in operation on January 1, 1933, was 110,700,000 tons per annum ; the capacity of the mines under construction was 142,300,000.

During the Second Five-Year Plan, 178 mines with a capacity of output of 143,000,000 tons are to be set into operation as against 179 pits with an output capacity of 56,900,000 tons set into operation during the First Piatiletka. Taking into account spent mines, the total output capacity of the mines in operation in 1937 is estimated to amount to 221,000,000 tons annually.

Of the 152·5 million tons total estimated output in 1937, about 113·5 million tons or 75·5 per cent. are to be produced in the new or capitally reconstructed pits set into operation in the First and Second Piatiletkas. In the Donetz district this proportion will be as high as 90 per cent.

Capital investments are to total 3,500,000,000 roubles as against 1,814,000,000 roubles in the First Piatiletka.

The Second Piatiletka provides for a very considerable increase in the mechanization of the pits. By 1937 coal cutting operations are to be 93·5 per cent. mechanized (as against 65·5 per cent. in 1932) ; hauling, 90 per cent. (as against 63·0 per cent. in 1932) ; underground conveying, 80 per cent. (15 per cent. in 1932) ; and so on. About 60 per cent. of all work at the pit surface is to be mechanized. If these plans are carried out the U.S.S.R. coal industry will become the most highly mechanized in the world.

Oil.

The progress of the oil industry even before, and particularly during, the First Piatiletka is well known. In the Second Piatiletka, in view of the greatly increased demand at home by aviation, motor cars, tractors, &c., the oil industry is to receive further rapid development.

Whilst output in the old oil fields is to be stimulated very considerably, special efforts are to be made to develop new fields outside the Caucasus. Among these may be mentioned the Lok-Batan, Kala, Karagkhur, Sulu-Tepe, and Kergez in the Azneft area ; Malgobek, Kayakent, Gornochechensk in the Grozneft area ; the Black Sea district in the Maineft area ; Kosh-Chagil, Shubar-Kubuk, S. Iskin, Sagiz, and Baichunoe in the Emba area ; Sterlitamak in the Eastern Oil area, &c.

Particularly important is the discovery of oil in the Ural region, where huge new industries are being developed. This will save the expense of transporting Baku oil to the East. In 1932 it was already obvious that the entire western slope of the Urals, from the Caspian to the Arctic, not only showed traces of oil, but that it was one of the richest oil-bearing districts in the world. The region from Emba to Sterlitamak (150,000 sq. kms.) alone is estimated to contain about 400 million tons of oil.

Sterlitamak oil is of excellent quality ; it has a high gasoline content, and a specific gravity of 0·905. It is possible to exploit commercially the whole triangle, whose corners may be roughly indicated at Chusovo-Sterlitamak-Samara bend (on the Volga).

Bashkiria is estimated to contain about 100 million tons of oil, with about 30 per cent. of gasoline.

Until 1932 the oilfields of Turkmenistan were considered of no importance, but the spouting gushers which became active in that year completely changed the reputation of this region. At the beginning of 1933 a gusher started at well No. 13 while it was being drilled, which gave over 10,000 tons of oil a day.

Oil has been discovered in the Fergan valley in Southern Uzbekistan and Tadjikistan, which will probably make Fergan valley the chief oil base for Central Asia.

Recent surveys in the Yakut Republic indicate that the entire area along the middle section of the Lena River and the Vilui River and its tributaries may become one of the great oil regions of the country.

In Saghalien, where hitherto oil had been found only on the Eastern and Western coasts, new oil deposits were discovered in 1931, some 30 kms. from the shores of the Sea of Okhotsk, similar to those in the Okha fields.

The total output of crude oil and gas in 1937 is estimated at 46,800,000 tons, as compared with 22,272,000 tons in 1932.

Some 40,000,000 tons of oil are to be refined in 1937, the following being the approximate output of the main distillates :

	1932. Tons.	1937. Tons.
Benzine	2,464,000	6,750,000
Ligroin	417,000	1,800,000
Kerosene	3,560,000	7,800,000
Lubricating oil . . .	782,000	2,000,000
Motor oil	1,250,000	4,500,000
Mazut	10,429,000	12,000,000

New refineries with up-to-date equipment, cracking plants, &c., are to be constructed, particularly on the Volga.

It is estimated that in the course of the Second Piatiletka some 11,700,000 metres (including prospecting both in new and old oil fields) will be drilled, as compared with 2,543,000 metres drilled during the First Piatiletka. Some 4,000 kms. of new pipe lines are to be laid during the

Five-Year period, among these being the lines Emba-Orsk, Nikitovka-Dnieper, Grozny-Armavir, Makhach-Kala-Voronezh, &c.

Capital investments in the oil industry during the five years will amount to 4,700,000,000 roubles, as against 1,446,000,000 roubles invested in the First Piatiletka.

Peat.

The output of peat is to increase from 13,302,000 tons in 1932 to 25,000,000 tons in 1937. The proportion of the output raised by mechanized means will increase from 49·7 per cent. in 1932 to 71·2 per cent. in 1937.

Capital investments by the Commissariat for Heavy Industries will amount to 600,000,000 roubles, as against 398,000,000 roubles invested in the First Piatiletka.

Shale.

The output of shale is to increase from 193,000 tons in 1932 to 2,600,000 tons in 1937. Eight new large shale mines, with a total capacity of output of 5,300,000 tons, are to be sunk during the Second Piatiletka. Six of these, with a total capacity of 3,400,000 tons, are to be set into operation in the course of the Second Piatiletka.

IRON AND STEEL

It is hoped during the Second Piatiletka to put an end to the lag in the rate of development of the ferrous metals, as compared with other important branches of the national economy. During the First Piatiletka the problem of creating a new powerful iron and steel industry, of replacing the former antiquated methods of work on small, poorly equipped units by the use of the most up-to-date and complicated machinery, of replacing the old technique of the nineteenth century by the latest American technique, presented extreme difficulties.

Enormous material resources were expended on the construction of new metallurgical giants in formerly uninhabited regions. The difficulties of building new plants and of reconstructing old ones without stopping work in them, and particularly the difficulties experienced by the masses of new workers and young engineers in mastering the advanced technique, accounted for the fact that during the last two years of the First Piatiletka the output of metal did not increase so rapidly as had been envisaged in the Plan.

The mastering of the huge, newly created and highly technical industrial apparatus demanded more time than would have been required if small works, small blast furnaces, and open hearth furnaces of the old type had been built. This explains why the iron and steel industry lagged behind the figures set for it by the Five-Year Plan, particularly in the output of steel and rolled metal.

One of the main problems of the Second Piatiletka is the mastery of the up-to-date equipment installed in the First Piatiletka, and to be installed in the Second Piatiletka. During the Second Piatiletka, the construction of a powerful metallurgical base in the Eastern parts of the U.S.S.R., started in the First Piatiletka, is to be completed.

The new works to be constructed are given under 'New Constructions.' It may be pointed out here that, in all, during the Second Piatiletka, there are to be constructed and set into operation 45 blast furnaces, 152 martens ovens, 3 converting sections, 107 rolling mills (including 13 bloomings), 13 pipe rolling mills, 4 pipe-welding aggregates, and a large number of electrical ovens, of tube foundry aggregates, &c. A large number of the old works are to be fundamentally reconstructed.

It is interesting to observe that of the total output of metals in 1937, the share to be produced by the new equipment installed during the Second Piatiletka will be 50·2 per cent. of the output of pig-iron and 41·5 per cent. of the output of steel, and if we include the output of the new and completely re-equipped plants during the First Piatiletka, the proportions will be 72 per cent. of pig-iron and 67 per cent. of steel.

The increase in the relative proportions of the total productions of pig-iron and of rolled metal in the Eastern metallurgical regions (including Urals, Central Volga,

Bashkiria, and Western Siberia) is illustrated by the following table :

District.	Pig-iron.			Rolled Metal.		
	Proportion Per Cent.					
	1927–8.	1932.	1937.	1927–8.	1932.	1937.
South .	73·0	69·9	58·1	66·4	63·5	55·9
Centre .	5·6	6·1	8·5	11·4	19·7	10·3
East .	21·4	24·0	33·4	22·2	16·8	33·8

Whilst the total industrial output in 1937 is estimated to be a little over twice that in 1932, the output of rolled metal is to be over three times.

During the First Piatiletka the main aim of the metallurgical industry was the supply of metal for the machine industry—in the Second Piatiletka this supply will be continued, but special attention is to be paid to the supply of metals for other branches of the national economy, particularly for transport. Thus the output of high quality rails is to increase from 326,000 tons in 1932, to about 1,400,000 tons in 1937, i.e. quadruple. Similarly, other branches of transport, agriculture, the timber industry, &c., are to receive a larger proportion of the home metals output than they obtained in the course of the First Piatiletka.

During the five years the Soviet metallurgical plants will require a total of some 200,000 tons of metal rolling and tube rolling equipment, as against 30,000 tons of such equipment installed during 1932 and 1933. The production of such equipment was only started in the U.S.S.R. in 1931, and the output is to be multiplied several times during 1933-7 in the Novoi Kramatorsk, Urals Machine Construction Plant, the Izhor, and other works.

The production of special iron and steel was started during the First Piatiletka, and in 1932, 555,000 tons of special rolled steel were produced. In 1937, however, the output of the latter is estimated at 2,100,000 tons and will form 15 per cent. of the total output of rolled metal, of which 6 per cent. will be rolled alloy steel (as compared with 6·3 per cent. in the U.S.A.).

Among the special steels now produced on a large scale in the U.S.S.R. are the following : different kinds of structural chrome, chrome nickel, chrome-molybdenum, chrome-vanadium steel, the production of steel for ball-bearings, sheet steel for transformers, high-speed steel, stainless steel, and heat-resisting steel, manganese and silicon steels, &c. The production of electrical steel in 1937 is estimated to amount to 600,000 tons (as against 115,000 tons in 1932), being second only to the U.S.A. (967,000 tons).

In general it is proposed during the five years to double the productive capacity of the metallurgical industry and to develop the production of various forms of metal—high-grade metal, electro-steel, ferro alloys, and so on, in dimensions fully satisfying the needs of the national economy. It is also proposed to carry through a wide reconstruction of the iron ore industry, introducing extensively the methods of concentrating ores.

Production in the U.S.S.R. is being more and more concentrated ; thus in 1937, works with capacity of output of over 600,000 tons of pig-iron will produce 75 per cent. of the total output (in 1932, such works gave only 10·3 per cent.). In 1937 there will be seven works, each with an output capacity of over 1,000,000 tons of pig-iron, and six works with an output capacity of over 1,000,000 tons steel each.

It is estimated that during the Five-Year period the productivity of labour will rise by 104 per cent., the output of pig-iron per worker per year is to increase from 235 tons in 1932 to 755 tons in 1937.

Non-Ferrous Metals and Rare Elements

Especially rapid rates of development and of technical re-equipment are, it is hoped, to be secured in the production of the non-ferrous metals which have rather lagged behind other industries.

A decided effort is to be made to effect a final transition to the modern method of obtaining copper (flotation and by reverberatory furnaces) and to introduce widely the advanced electrolytic method in the production of zinc, obtaining 70 per cent. of the output of this metal by this method in 1937. It is also proposed to organize the production of tin, nickel, magnesium, and greatly to develop the production of aluminium ; an endeavour is to be made, as far as possible, to satisfy completely the requirements of the entire national economy of non-ferrous metals by increasing their output.

By 1937 it is estimated that the output of copper will be 155,000 tons ; lead, 120,000 tons ; zinc, 100,000 tons ; and aluminium, 80,000 tons. The U.S.S.R. is rich in all these metals, particularly rich deposits of bauxite of very high grade have been discovered comparatively recently in the Urals, where big aluminium works are to be constructed.

Manganese.

The U.S.S.R. is also very rich in manganese, of which it is estimated that it possesses about 588,700,000 tons, i.e. 65 per cent. of the known resources of the world. The output of manganese is estimated to increase from about 830,000 tons in 1932 to 2,700,000 tons in 1937.

Gold.

The gold districts in the Urals and Siberia are being developed as rapidly as possible and, in addition, a number of new goldfields are now being exploited. Among them should be noted such rich and promising regions as Aldan (Yakutia). Other new districts are Darasun and Bolei, Rich gold deposits have also been discovered in Kazakstan, Northern Caucasus, and Tadjikistan.

Scientific expeditions and prospecting parties are constantly at work looking for new gold-bearing districts throughout the vast territory of the U.S.S.R. The gold discovered in the last two years in the Altai surpass the deposits known before the war in the entire Eastern Siberian region.

In the course of an interview with the correspondent of the *New York Times*, December 25, 1933, M. Stalin said :

' Our gold output is already more than double the output of Tsarist days, and yields at the present time over 100,000,000 roubles annually. During the past two years we have particularly improved the methods of our prospecting work, and have discovered large deposits.

' But our industry is yet young. This is true, not only of gold mining, but also of iron, steel, copper, and metallurgical industry as a whole. Our young industry is not yet strong enough to aid sufficiently our gold industry. Our tempo of development is rapid, but its volume is still not large. We could quadruple our gold output within a short time had we more dredges and other machinery.'

The immense deposits of complex ores in the Altai Mountains (Kazakstan) are so rich in gold (30 to 80 grammes per ton) that they should be regarded primarily as sources of gold rather than of non-ferrous metals.

The extent of mechanization of the gold industry was over 70 per cent. in 1933 (in 1913 only 20 per cent. of the whole gold industry was mechanized). The total number of dredges, both steam and electric, amounted to 85 at the end of 1933. The dredges manufactured by the Putilov Works are capable of an output of 3,500 cubic metres of rock per day.

Already in 1933 the Soviet Union is said to have occupied second place in the world production, and has surpassed both the U.S.A. (2,750,000 ounces) and Canada (2,961,000 ounces).

It is a fact, recognized by all gold experts, that the gold deposits of the Soviet Union exceed by far those of South Africa or any other country.

While in pre-war Russia, ore or vein-gold constituted only 15 per cent. of the total production, in 1932 it constituted about one-third.

Rare Elements.

During the First Five-Year Plan a beginning was made with the production of the rare elements—radium, tungsten, vanadium, molybdenum, beryllium, selenium, cadmium, titanium, mercury, also platinum, nickel, &c.—all of which are found in the U.S.S.R. (in Trans-Baikal, Transcaucasia, Central Asia, Kirghiz, &c.). In the Second Piatiletka their output is to be greatly increased.

CHEMICAL INDUSTRY

The Soviet chemical industry was built up entirely during the First Five-Year Plan period, and is served by the most up-to-date technique.

During the Second Piatiletka, it has been resolved to secure decided advances in the development of the chemical industry, ensuring the utilization of chemical processes wherever possible in all branches of the national economy and a strengthening of the defensive power of the country. The production of all forms of chemical fertilizers is to be raised tenfold during the years of the Second Five-Year Plan. It is proposed to develop the utilization of a variety of new chemical processes such as the chemical reworking of hard fuel—coal, peat, slate, the production of new forms of dyes, synthetic rubber, and so on ; to introduce the latest technological processes in the chemical industry (extensive development of electro-thermic and electrolytic methods, to carry through reactions in gaseous phases, the use of catalysers at high pressure and temperatures, of biochemical processes, and so on) ; to promote the combination of the chemical industry with other branches of industry (coke, non-ferrous metallurgy, iron, and so on) and the introduction of a number of new forms of raw material.

The value of the gross output of the chemical industry is estimated to increase from 1·5 milliard roubles in 1932 to 4·5 milliard roubles in 1937 (in 1926–7 prices). Thus, during the Five-Year period, output will be about trebled, but the output of heavy chemicals is to be six times that in 1932.

Particularly interesting is the development of the rubber industry. During the First Five-Year Plan period, the rubber industry was radically reconstructed and became a large-scale industry, not to be compared with the pre-revolutionary comparatively small rubber enterprises.

The great technical equipment thus supplied enabled the rubber industry to complete its Five-Year Plan in three years. The output of rubber technical goods in 1932 increased 89·3 per cent. as compared with 1913, and 300 per cent. as compared with 1928.

In 1937 the output of rubber footwear is to increase from 64,800,000 pair in 1932 to 120,000,000 pair; rubber soles from 14,000 tons to 30,000 tons; the number of tyres produced will be 3,000,000, over five times that produced in 1932.

The manufacture of plastics, used for a variety of purposes in industry, and only started on a large scale during the First Piatiletka, is scheduled to increase by 1937, twelve times as compared with 1932.

New works for the manufacture of synthetic rubber are to be constructed and the production of fine chemicals, medicaments, and other branches of the chemical industry is to be greatly extended.

Side by side with the extension of already existing enterprises, chemical works are to be erected in a number of other districts where they can be combined with other industries, or where the by-products of the latter can form valuable raw materials for the chemical industry : thus, aniline dye works and lacquer dye works are to be established in the Eastern districts, the Urals and Western Siberia ; shale chemical works in the Chuvash Republic ; new soda works at Karabugaz, Iletskaya Zashchita, and Western Siberia ; iodine works are to be erected in the districts bordering on the Caspian Sea, &c.

BUILDING MATERIALS

The total value of the output of building materials is estimated to increase from 711,000,000 roubles in 1932 to 1,659,000,000 roubles in 1937 (at 1926–7 prices in each case).

The principal materials produced and to be produced are :

	1932.	1937.
Cement (tons) . . .	3,489,000	7,500,000
Fire bricks (tons) . . .	793,000	2,300,000
Dinas ,, (,,) . . .	178,000	800,000
Asbestos (,,) . . .	59,900	200,000
Bricks (number) . . .	4,736,000,000	8,000,000,000

The capital to be invested during the Second Piatiletka by the Commissariat for Heavy Industries (which is responsible for about three-quarters of the total output of the building materials industries) is fixed at about 1,501,000,000 roubles.

About 600,000,000 roubles is to be invested during the five years in the construction of special works for the production of fire-resisting materials. Among the new works for the production of high-quality fire-resisting materials to be constructed are the Chelyabinsk and Zaporozh Plants.

In the building materials industry as in other industries, new works are to be constructed in the various national Republics and areas such as Yakutsk Republic, Mari area, Eastern Siberia, Far East, Murmansk, Kazakstan, Central Asia, also in the Urals, Eastern Asia, Transcaucasia, &c.

Every effort is to be employed to utilize local raw material and to mechanize the production of local building materials.

TIMBER AND WOODWORKING

During the First Piatiletka, the U.S.S.R. began to exploit the vast timber regions of the Far East, Siberia, and Far North, thus also shifting the sphere of woodworking to these future centres of the timber industry. The fulfilment of the Second Piatiletka is bound up with the development of the timber resources of the Northern and Eastern regions of the Union.

The Urals, Northern, Gorki, and Far Eastern areas and Eastern and Western Siberia together accounted for 46·2 per cent. of the timber collected and forwarded in 1932 ; in 1937 these districts are to account for 59·3 per cent. of such timber. On the other hand, the proportion of timber to be obtained from the Central districts (Moscow and Western districts, Central Black Earth area, Central Volga, Ukraine, and White Russia) is to be reduced from 29·3 per cent. in 1932 to 16·5 per cent. in 1937.

The Northern Caucasus and Transcaucasia are to increase their output two and a half times and Yakutsk over seven times.

The quantity of timber worked up in the saw mills and the wood-working industries in 1937 are scheduled to increase by over 78 per cent. as compared with 1932.

The amount of industrial wood consumed by the paper industry is estimated to double during the Five-Year period. The quantity of pit props supplied to the coal mines in 1937 should be 3·5 times that in 1932.

The measures already started in the First Piatiletka for the mechanization of all branches of the timber and wood-working industry are to be greatly extended. Among other things, the chief timber collection processes are to be mechanized ; mechanization of the moving of logs from forest to mill is to be increased six times and milling processes three times ; charcoal burning is to be mechanized.

Capital Investments by the Commissariat for Timber will total some 950,000,000 roubles, of which 444,000,000 roubles are to be spent in mechanizing timber forwarding ; 153,500,000 roubles for mechanizing timber floating ; 206,800,000 roubles for housing of timber workers and 145,700,000 roubles for other work.

The quantity of sawn timber to be produced in 1937 is estimated at 43,000,000 cubic metres as against 24,470,000 cubic metres in 1932, an increase of 18,500,000 cubic metres. Of this quantity, 7,000,000 cubic metres are to be obtained from mills, the construction of which will be started during the Second Five-Year Plan, whilst the rest of the increase—11,500,000 cubic metres—is to be obtained in the mills, the construction of which was started in the First Piatiletka, and also from the improved exploitation of the mills already in operation.

It is estimated that building will consume over 18,000,000 cubic metres of sawn timber in 1937 as compared with 9·1 million cubic metres in 1932, the quantity consumed by such industries as carriage, truck and motor construction, &c., will increase from 7·5 million cubic metres in 1932 to 13·35 million cubic metres in 1937, whilst the industries catering for general household needs (furniture, &c.) are to receive 2,400,000 cubic metres of sawn timber in 1937 as against 730,000 cubic metres in 1932.

Thus the value of the output of furniture by the enterprises of the Timber Commissariat is estimated to increase from 73,900,000 roubles in 1932 to 250,000,000 roubles in 1937 (in 1926–7 prices), whilst the timber co-operatives are estimated to produce in 1937 200,000,000 roubles' worth of furniture as against 109,500,000 roubles' worth in 1932 (in 1932 planned prices).

In order to increase the output of articles and parts required by various branches of industry and building organizations, the Plan provides for the construction in the Second Piatiletka of saw mills in the form of combined enterprises, containing sections for the further working up of the lumber materials. The Plan also provides for the construction of temporary timber works with movable sawing frames in various timber areas as required.

In the plywood industry thirteen new works are to be constructed, of which six will be set into operation in the course of the Five-Year period. The total output of plywood is to increase from 423,500 cubic metres in 1932 to 735,000 cubic metres in 1937.

The Timber Commissariat will invest in its various woodworking construction works during the Second Piatiletka some 1,140,000,000 roubles.

Amongst other things, the Plan provides for the re-afforestation during the five years of some 141,500 hectares, at a cost of about 20,900,000 roubles.

It also provides for measures of water preservation in the Volga, Dnieper, and Don River basins. Along the banks of these rivers artificial afforestation is to be carried out during the five years, over an area of about 476,100 hectares.

On these and other forestry measures it is proposed to spend about 109,000,000 roubles. For surveying and research work, the Timber Commissariat is to spend about 67,200,000 roubles during the five years.

The Plan also provides for increasing the manufacture of various chemical products from wood and wood waste, the capital expenditure for this purpose being fixed at 214,000,000 roubles.

THE LIGHT AND FOOD INDUSTRIES

As has been stated in the Introduction, the fundamental aim of the Second Piatiletka is to raise the standard of life of the workers and peasants of the U.S.S.R. For this purpose it is necessary to raise the quantity and quality of the output of the light and food industries, and this is the more possible now that the First Piatiletka has largely solved the problem of the industrialization of the country by the building up of a powerful heavy industry and the organization of large-scale agriculture. Hence the tasks of the Second Piatiletka in respect of the light and food industries are officially set out as follows :

To develop in every way the most important branches of the light and food industries by mechanizing them as far as possible. For instance, there is to be an increase in the proportion of automatic weaving looms in the cotton industry up to 40 per cent. at the end of the Second Five-Year Plan, and obsolete looms are to be replaced by up-to-date machines.

To liquidate the technical backwardness of the linen industry by the introduction of high-speed machines and the radical reconstruction of the primary preparation of flax.

To effect an all-round mechanization of knitted fabric, clothing, and footwear production.

To establish a large-scale mechanized meat industry on the basis of the development of combine enterprises.

To increase the proportion of mechanized fishing to 70 per cent. of the catch of the State fishing industry by a considerable reconstruction of the fishing fleet.

To reconstruct the vegetable oil industry by the introduction of the most effective extraction method of production.

To increase the classifications of yarn and to improve greatly the quality of cotton and linen ; to raise the proportion of fine cloths and the worsted groups of the woollen industry ; to raise the proportion of the fine wool in fabrics.

To improve the quality of soap by a greater use of fats ; to improve the quality of footwear, both in methods of sewing and in the use of improved quality of raw material.

To improve the quality of products of the meat industry by raising the proportion of ham, sausage, and food fats ; to improve the quality of production in the fishing industry by increasing the proportion of the better kinds of fish ; to increase considerably the quality and assortment of the output of the flour milling industry by raising the proportion of best products.

Capital investment in the light industries during the Second Piatiletka will amount to 16,100,000,000 roubles as compared with 3,500,000,000 roubles in the First Piatiletka. The value of the output of the light industries is to increase from 7,800,000,000 roubles in 1932 to 19,500,000,000 roubles in 1937.

Amongst other increases may be mentioned articles required by clubs, libraries, schools, &c., the output of which, in 1937, is estimated to be treble that in 1932. The output of the paper industry is to be more than doubled, the output of pencils, paints, pens, exercise books, &c., is to increase about three and a half times, and the output of musical instruments will be more than quadrupled.

The Plan provides for the more rational exploitation of existing enterprises and equipment, and also for the construction of new enterprises and equipment. New textile bases are being constructed in Western Siberia, Central Asia, and Transcaucasia, whilst the Ukraine is being converted into a large-scale textile area by the construction of new large works.

In the Urals, important earthenware and glass manufacturing works are to be constructed, &c.

Over the U.S.S.R., as a whole, 15 powerful cotton combinats, 13 wool mills, 12 linen factories, 11 hemp enterprises, 18 knitting mills, 21 boot and shoe works, 52 clothing factories are to be constructed.

New types of equipment, including automatic looms in the weaving sections of the cotton and woollen industries and new types of spinning frames in the cotton industry are being introduced.

Similarly, new and improved equipment is being introduced in the linen, hemp, and jute industries where new spinning frames of Soviet invention are being brought into exploitation.

It is claimed that by 1937 various branches of the light industries of the U.S.S.R. will take first place in Europe, and second in the world.

As a result of the development of agriculture, the value of the supply of raw materials for the food industry is scheduled to more than double during the Five-Year period.

Considerable work is to be carried out in mechanizing and extending various branches of the food industry (canning, refrigerating, creameries, bakeries, &c.), as well as constructing new modern enterprises.

The total capital investments during the Five-Year period by the Commissariat for Supply is calculated at 5,340,000,000 roubles as against 1,858,000,000 roubles in the First Piatiletka, whilst the Committee for Collections (of the flour, milling, and cereals industry) is to invest 550,000,000 roubles as against 153,000,000 roubles in the First Piatiletka. Of the total capital investment in the food industries, 2,820,000,000 roubles are to be spent on entirely new constructions, including the completion of enterprises, the construction of which was started in the course of the First Piatiletka.

TRANSPORT AND COMMUNICATIONS

As was pointed out in the summary of the First Five-Year Plan, considerable difficulty was occasioned as a result of the inability of the transport system of the U.S.S.R., in spite of the very real progress made during this period, to cope with the demands of the boisterously developing national economy of the country as a whole.

The Second Five-Year Plan accordingly sets itself the task of the further development and reconstruction of transport, special attention being concentrated on mastering modern railway technique as well as the technique of other forms of transport.

A total of 26,500,000,000 roubles are to be invested in the development of transport.

The Plan lays down the following estimates regarding goods and passenger traffic of the principal forms of transport:

	Goods. (Milliard Ton Kms.)		Passengers. (Million Persons.)	
	1932.	1937.	1932.	1937.
Railways . .	169	300	966·6	1,309·5
River . .	36	63	48·5	78·0
Marine . .	18	51	3·7	6·2
Motor . .	1·1	16	—	—
Air . . .	—	—	0·03	1·5

The quantity of goods transported by air in 1937 is estimated to amount to 15,000 tons (as against 447 tons in 1932), whilst the air post is estimated to carry 36,000 tons of postal packages in 1937 (as against 430 in 1932). Similar progress is to be made in the utilization of aviation in agriculture, forestry, surveying, and scientific expeditions of all kinds. It is estimated that some 6,000,000 hectares will be sown by air in 1937.

Railways.

It is estimated that the Commissariat for Transport will invest 17,500,000,000 roubles in railway development during the Five-Year period, of which 10,000,000,000 roubles are to be spent on the reconstruction and extension of the existing railway system and 2,700,000,000 roubles on new constructions, the rest being spent on capital repairs, renovations and housing.

Among the most important measures of construction and reconstruction are the following :

The reconstruction of the most important railroad lines ; electrification of 5,000 kms. of track ; the laying of 9,500 kms. of auxiliary track on those trunk systems experiencing the worst congestion of traffic (e.g. the Ural-Kuzbas, the Trans-Baikal, the Ussurisk and Donbas railroads, &c.) ; the increasing of the length of station lines by 8,500 kms. ; the replacing of light by heavy rails over a length of 20,000 kms. ; bridge building ; the installation of automatic signalling over a distance of 8,300 kms. ; the strengthening of the existing tracks by the use of metal ballast and by increasing the number of sleepers per kilometre of track and so on.

The increase of the number of locomotives from 19,500 in 1932 to 24,600 in 1937, with a simultaneous transition to more powerful, more up-to-date types of locomotive (the powerful railroad engine ' FD ' is to become the chief locomotive for goods traffic, and the powerful railroad engine ' JS ' the main locomotive for passenger trains) ; the more extensive use of internal combustion and electric locomotives.

Increasing the number of railroad carriages from 552,000 in 1932 to 800,000 in 1937 (on a two-axle basis) ; considerably increasing the proportion of large freight cars ; the equipment of all cars with automatic brakes, not less than half to be equipped with automatic coupling devices.

Automatic block signalling is to be spread over a distance of 8,300 kms., as against the 582 kms. of block signalling at the end of the First Piatiletka. The total length of new big metal bridges alone to be built during the Second Five-Year Plan is estimated to total over 25 kms.

The construction of the largest new railroad lines : Baikal-Amur, Akmolinsk-Kartaly, Moscow-Donbas, Karaganda-Balkhash, Ufa-Magnitnaya, and other railroads, increasing the total length of railroad lines from 83,300 kms. on January 1, 1933 to 94,000 kms. on January 1, 1938. (In 1913 the total length of railway was 58,500 kms.), thus adding over 10,000 kms. of new lines during the Five-Year period.

Speaking of the Baikal-Amur line, at the Communist Party Congress in February 1934, Molotov, Chairman of the Council of People's Commissaries, said :

> ' The construction of the Baikal-Amur line over a distance of 1,400 kms. stands out by its greatness among all new railroad constructions. It will connect the Transbaikal with the Lower Amur, and will assist in drawing into economic life a large territory hitherto largely inaccessible to man.'

During 1934 it is expected that the following railroads will be opened to traffic : Karaganda-Balkhash (350 kms.) ; Tomsk-Chulym (95 kms.) ; Grishino-Pavlograd (114 kms.) ; Zolotonosha-Mironovka ; some parts of the Black Sea Railroad in Transcaucasia.

The total length of new rails to be laid down during the Second Piatiletka will be as follows :

New lines (mostly double tracks) . 10,000 kms.
Second tracks   .   .   . 9,500 ,,
Station lines   .   .   . 8,500 ,,
Renewal lines   .   .   . 40,000 ,, (linear)

Calculated in linear kms., this signifies the laying down of over 100,000 kms. of new rails.

Moreover, whereas only 2 per cent. of the rails laid down up to the end of the First Five-Year Plan had a weight of 43 kgs. per linear metre and 28 per cent. had a weight below 33 kgs. per linear metre, it is proposed in future to use in main line construction and when renewing rails only the heaviest rail with a weight of 44 kgs. per metre. This will ensure longer service and make the railroads capable of withstanding the heavier types of locomotives and rolling stock.

As a result of this development the U.S.S.R. will have three double-track powerful main lines from the centre to the east, instead of as at present three single-track lines ; she will have four double-track main lines from the centre southwards and one double-track main line from the Donbas eastwards.

All this, it is hoped, will lead to a better organization of transport in the Ural-Kuzbas area, and of railroad connexion between the centre of the U.S.S.R. and Middle Asia.

By 1937 sections of railroads carrying most freight are scheduled to be electrified. Large tracts of railways passing through the Donetz and Dnieper Basins, Murmansk, and Transcaucasia, as well as sections in parts of the Urals and Northern Caucasus, will thus be electrified.

There is also to be a considerable development in the electrification of the suburban passenger lines of Moscow, Leningrad, Kharkov, and Mineralnye Vody.

Railway stations and repair shops are also to be supplied more plentifully with electrical energy. The total consumption of electricity by railway transport is estimated to increase from 300,000,000 kw. hours in 1932 to about 1,600,000,000 kw. hours in 1937.

River and Marine Transport.

A gigantic programme of construction of artificial water routes is to be carried through as follows : the Baltic-White Sea Canal to a length of 227 kms. (the first part was finished in 1933—the first year of the Second Five-Year Plan) ; the Moscow-Volga Canal, 127 kms. in length ; the Volga-Don Canal, 100 kms. long, and the reconstruction of the Mariinsk and Moscow River water systems, which, with the large volume of hydro-technical works on the existing water routes (the through route on the Dnieper, the construction of sluices on the river Sozh, the reconstruction of the Middle Volga) will, in the main, ensure the reconstruction of the waterways and the formation of a unified water system in the European part of the U.S.S.R., uniting the White, Baltic, Black, and Caspian Seas.

The length of navigable waterways should increase in the Second Five-Year Plan from 84,000 kms. to 101,000 kms., with a considerable improvement in conditions of navigation.

The maritime and river fleet is to be radically renovated and reconstructed, and the construction of small draft vessels for utilization on small rivers is to be developed. The merchant fleet, in general, will be considerably renovated, and the average age of the vessels used will be reduced from twenty-eight to thirty in 1932, to fifteen to seventeen years in 1937.

Motor Transport.

In motor road transport, the number of automobiles is to increase from 75,000 on January 1, 1933 to 580,000 on January 1, 1938, or almost eightfold ; the construction of a network of unpaved and paved highroads is to be developed widely, thus, in the main, abolishing roadlessness ; the total length of roads in the country is to be increased by 210,000 kms. This is exclusive of the considerable construction to be carried out by localities at their own expense.

Capital investments in road-building during the Five Years is to be treble the sum so invested in the First Piatiletka, and is fixed at 2,960,000,000 roubles (exclusive of local contributions), of which 1,960,000,000 roubles is to be devoted to new road constructions and reconstructions.

Decided advances are to be achieved in the mechanization of loading and unloading work in transport, with a threefold growth in mechanization on the railways from 18 to 57 per cent., in maritime transport from 14 to 72 per cent., and in river transport from 12 to 56 per cent., i.e. approximately a fivefold increase.

The Plan seeks to increase the productivity of labour in the Second Five-Year Plan by 43 per cent. on the railways and 86 per cent. in water transport, and estimates a fall in the net costs of exploitation of all forms of transport by 40 per cent., including 10·5 per cent. on the railways, 36 per cent. in water transport, and 54 per cent. in motor transport.

Air Transport.

In the civil air fleet, the network of air lines of All-Union importance is to increase in the Second Five-Year Plan from nearly 32,000 to 85,000 kms., i.e. almost three-fold. Side by side with this, the construction of local air lines is to be extensively developed, bringing up their length to 35,000 kms. in 1937 (see also p. 74).

About 1,207,000,000 roubles are to be invested during the Five Years in civil aviation, as against 246,000,000 roubles so invested in the First Piatiletka.

The achievements of Soviet civil aviation are well known, particularly the heroic work of the aviators who carried out the rescue of the Cheluskin expedition which had been wrecked on the Arctic ice, also the Soviet record stratosphere flights, &c.

Communications.

The various branches of the postal services (post, telegraph, telephone, radio), on the whole, are to more than double their operations during the Five-Year period.

There is to be a wide-scale development of all types of communication, particularly radio, and it is hoped to bring about a fundamental improvement in the quality of the services.

Capital investments in the postal services (excluding radio) is to amount to 1,700,000,000 roubles as compared with 565,000,000 roubles invested in the First Piatiletka.

AGRICULTURE

In the course of the First Five-Year Plan, Soviet agriculture was transformed from small-scale farming by private peasants into large-scale farming in collectives (kolkhozy) and in State farms (sovkhozy). The kulaks (peasant profiteers) have been practically extinguished as a class, although the psychology of the kulak and of the small peasant proprietor has not yet completely vanished from the Soviet villages.

The Second Piatiletka aims at completing the process of collectivization, so that every working peasant is either a member of a kolkhoz or is working in a sovkhoz, at the complete extinction of the kulaks as a class and the total substitution of large-scale for small-scale agriculture.

The Plan provides for the further mechanization of agriculture (which has been made possible by the progress of the Soviet heavy industries) and for the application to agriculture of the most scientific methods. This in its turn will enable the realization of the ultimate aim of all these measures—the raising of the standard of life of the peasantry, to make every member of the kolkhozy—in the words of M. Stalin—into ' a well-to-do peasant ' ; i.e. into a well-to-do peasant, who will live a comfortable cultured existence without the possibility of exploiting other peasants.

During the Second Piatiletka the total value of the agricultural produce is estimated to increase from 13·1 milliard roubles in 1932 to 26·5 milliard roubles in 1937 (1926–7 prices in each case), the rate of increase being an average of 15 per cent. annually. This is in striking contrast with the 2·9 per cent. annual rate of progress of agriculture in Germany in the period 1860–1913, and 1·7 per cent. in the U.S.A. during the famous ' prosperity ' period. The output of some branches of agriculture in 1937 is estimated as follows :

Grain crops—1,048 million centners, with a harvest yield of 10 centners per hectare.

Sugar-beet—276 million centners, with a harvest yield up to 200 centners per hectare.

Flax fibre—8 million centners, with a harvest yield of 3·7 centners per hectare.

Stock-breeding to be increased by two and a quarter times.

The area under Egyptian cotton is to increase from 51,000 hectares in 1932 to 230,000 hectares in 1937.

One of the main aims of the agricultural plan is to solve the grain question, i.e. to assure by the end of the Five-Year period, good stable harvests and to increase the proportion in the total harvest of the more valuable cultures.

There will not be any great extension in the sown area, and what extension there will be is to occur mostly in the so-called consuming areas, whilst the only culture which is to receive any great extension is wheat, the area under which is to increase from 34·5 million hectares in 1932 (both Spring and Autumn sowings) to over 40·8 million hectares in 1937.

It is estimated that in the consuming areas, the grain raised will increase from 159,000,000 centners in 1932 to 257,000,000 centners in 1937, whilst the production of wheat in these areas will increase from 3·8 million centners to 40 million centners.

The estimated increase in the grain raised is, in general, to be mainly the result of the improved methods of work. It is considered that the increased yield of grain will enable the average consumption of the latter per soul of population to be raised by about 20 per cent., whilst increasing the use of fodder for livestock to some 320 to 350 million centners, and raising the State reserves of grain by the end of 1937 to 300,000,000 centners.

If the Plan estimates are fulfilled, the U.S.S.R., in 1937, will take first place in the world with regard to the production of wheat, barley, oats, flax fibre, and sugar-beet, and will be second only to the U.S.A. in the production of raw cotton.

The following are the measures which the Plan considers necessary in order to place Soviet agriculture on this high level :

To transform grain, live-stock breeding, sugar-beet, cotton, and other State farms into model agricultural undertakings by a thorough mastery of the technique of modern complex machinery ; by introducing correct crop rotation and organizing the work of seed selection, cleansing, &c. ; by improving the breeds of cattle ; by raising the quality of output and increasing the supplies of grain, beet, cotton, meat, milk, butter, leather, and wool delivered to the Government.

To divide any unduly large State farms into smaller units, and to abolish excessive specialization.

To increase the number of machine tractor stations from 2,446 in 1932 to 6,000 in 1937, the machine tractor stations to serve all collective farms.

To increase the gross tractor power from 2,225,000 h.p. in 1932 to 8,200,000 h.p. in 1937—an increase of 370 per cent.

To increase the total number of combines to 100,000 as against 14,100 in 1932, and the number of automobiles in agriculture to 170,000, i.e. by over twelve times. It is estimated that the sovkhozy which are, of course, the most highly mechanized farms in the U.S.S.R. will have by 1937 a gross tractor power of about 3,400,000 h.p., about 27,000 combines and 58,000 motors.

To complete, in the main, the mechanization of agriculture : 80 per cent. of the ploughing and fallow ploughing in 1937 to be done by tractor, 70 per cent. of cultivation and 60 per cent. of reaping to be done by tractors and reaping machines ; threshing to be mechanized 85 per cent. With respect to the mechanization of agriculture the U.S.S.R. in 1937, it is estimated, will be first in the world.

To sow 75 per cent. of the grain area with cleaned seeds, 50 per cent. of the sowing area to be winter ploughed.

To raise the level of cotton-growing during the Second Five-Year Plan by increasing the area fertilized by nitrates from 6 per cent. to 80 per cent. ; in the case of sugar-beet to increase the area on which nitrate fertilization is used from 6 per cent. to 40 per cent. and to raise the area on which phosphorus fertilizers is employed from 9 per cent. to 100 per cent.

Irrigation to be extensively developed, the area irrigated to be increased by 1 million hectares.

The increase in the supply of mineral fertilizers for use in agriculture generally is estimated as follows :

	1932. Tons.	1937. Tons.
Nitrogenous fertilizers	52,800	1,760,000
Potassium fertilizers	79,000	1,680,000
Superphosphates	612,000	3,400,000
Flour of phosphate	396,000	2,900,000

6

It is also interesting to note that the plan makes provision for the considerable extension of the cultivation of a large variety of sub-tropical trees and plants, including a variety of rubber plants in the sub-tropical districts as well as in other southern areas of the U.S.S.R. An extensive programme of mechanization, drainage, and other meliorative measures is to be carried out in the sub-tropical districts, which it is hoped will ultimately provide a plentiful supply of many valuable industrial plants.

The area under tea is fixed to increase from 21,700 hectares in 1932 to 55,000 hectares in 1937 ; the gross quantity of raw tea leaves to be gathered increasing from 2,300 tons in 1932 to 48,600 tons in 1937.

The area under such sub-tropical fruits as mandarines, lemons, &c., will be trebled during the Five-Year period. The Plan also provided for a great increase in the areas under fruit, edible berries, vineyards, &c.

Apart from the cows and other livestock in the possession of individual members of kolkhozy which, too, it is expected, will increase enormously, the herds are to increase as follows :

	Sovkhozy. (Mill. heads at end of year.)		Kolkhoz. Stock-breeding Farms. (Mill. heads at end of year.)	
	1932.	1937.	1932.	1937.
Cows . .	1·65	2·4	1·88	4·05
Other big-horned cattle . .	1·55	3·8	3·42	4·45
Pigs . .	1·8	5·45	2·4	8·2
Sheep and goats	5·7	12·2	5·4	22·6

Like other branches of the national economy, agriculture is to be largely electrified.

The total supply of electric energy for agricultural purposes is expected to increase as follows :

	Power. (Thousand Kws.)		Electric Energy Supplied. (Million Kw. Hours.)	
	1932.	1937.	1932.	1937.
From small agricultural stations . .	53·0	180·0	74·0	300·0
From agricultural sub-stations of district electrical stations	12·9	245·0	21·0	500·0
Total .	65·9	425·0	95·0	800·0

Special efforts are to be made to electrify as far as possible such processes as threshing—electrical threshing stations are to be increased from 551 in 1932 to 15,000 in 1937. Electricity is to be used very widely for lighting and other purposes in all kinds of farms, including animal-breeding farms.

It is proposed to establish a number of experimental centres for the study of the electrification of agriculture in the Moscow, Ivanovo districts, the Urals, in the Crimea—Anap district, in the Northern Caucasus, and in the Dnieper Basin area.

It is estimated that a total of 21,900,000,000 roubles will be invested in socialized, i.e. Sovkhoz and Kolkhoz agriculture during the Second Piatiletka (as against 10·8 milliard roubles in the First Piatiletka). Of this sum, 16·9 milliard roubles will be invested by the State organizations, and 5 milliard roubles by the kolkhozy from their own accumulations. In addition, it is expected that members of kolkhozy will invest some 6·5 milliard roubles in developing their individually owned herds and in housing.

It is proposed to invest 7,192,000,000 roubles in the sovkhozy during the Five-Year period for the purpose of completing their mechanization, housing, and other constructions, thus doubling their basic capital as compared with 1932. Special attention is to be paid to the stock-breeding sovkhozy.

With the realization of the Second Piatiletka, it is estimated that the average kolkhoz member in 1937 will be considerably better off than the rich private peasant-farmer was in 1927. According to the 1927 census (and the estimates of the Second Piatiletka) and calculating in 1926–7 prices, the average value of the most important means of production per hectare sown at the disposal of a kolkhoz member in 1937 will be 184 roubles, as compared with 156 roubles of an average rich peasant in 1927.

The gross production (in 1926–7 prices) per soul of population in the Kolkhozy will be 181 roubles in 1937 as compared with 153 roubles in 1927 in a rich peasant farm, and the net income per soul of population will be 127 roubles in 1937 in the kolkhoz as compared with 83 roubles in a rich peasant family. In addition, it should be borne in mind that the kolkhoz farms have already and in 1937 will have, to a still greater extent, modern machinery, which even the kulak never had ; moreover, the opportunities of education and culture in the villages even now, and still more at the end of the Second Piatiletka, will be such as even the richest peasant could scarcely have hoped for formerly.

TECHNICAL TRAINING OF WORKERS

If the advances of the national economy outlined in the previous pages are to be realized, it will necessitate a great increase in the number of technicians and highly-skilled workers. The Plan, therefore, lays down an extensive programme in this direction.

During the course of the First Piatiletka, industry received an additional 300,000 skilled workers, and other branches of the national economy 150,000 such workers, who had been trained in the factory workshop training schools.

During the period of the Second Piatiletka, it is proposed to raise the qualification of some 5,000,000 persons, including 2,500,000 (1,700,000 for industry and 500,000 for transport) in the factory training schools; 1,500,000 trained (as tractorists, tractor mechanics, combine workers, leaders of brigades, &c.), in the specially organized agricultural schools and courses and also in the permanent schools for sovkhoz workers, and 700,000 in schools and courses for motor drivers, &c.

In addition, it is estimated that some tens of millions of workers and kolkhoz members are to attend various training and retraining courses during the Five-Year period.

About 340,000 specialists are scheduled to graduate from the universities during the Second Five-Year Plan as against the 170,700 during the First Five-Year Plan, a twofold increase, and 850,000 specialists are to graduate from the polytechnical colleges against 308,000 during the First Five-Year Plan, a threefold increase.

The number of qualified specialists in all branches of the national economy is estimated to increase from 2·7 million persons at the end of 1932 to 4,000,000 at the end of 1937, i.e. by 46·5 per cent., including a 57 per cent. increase in the number of specialists in industry, 60 per cent. in transport, posts and telegraphs, telephone and radio services, and 100 per cent. in agriculture. Expenditure for these purposes will reach some 24,400,000,000 roubles.

As a result, it is claimed that, by the end of 1937, the most important industries of the U.S.S.R. will have a higher proportion of specialists than is the case in Germany. Thus in the coal industry the proportion of experts is estimated to reach 6·0 per cent. (in Germany it is 4·2 per cent.) ; in the metallurgical industries, 10 per cent. (in Germany 6·2 per cent.) ; in the machine building industry, 12·1 per cent. (in Germany 9·8 per cent.).

It is also particularly interesting to note that not only is it proposed to raise the number and proportion of trained specialists in all branches of the national economy, but also to raise their qualifications, thus, the total number of specialists with a completed special secondary or university course of education is scheduled to increase from 1,400,000 in 1932 (49·9 per cent. of the total number of specialists) to 2,300,000 in 1937 (57·9 per cent. of the total number of specialists).

STANDARD OF LIFE OF WORKERS AND PEASANTS

Unemployment was abolished in the course of the First Piatiletka, and so far from any need to worry about unemployment, the Second Piatiletka envisages an increase in the number of workers and office employees at the end of the Five-Year Plan by 26 per cent. in all branches of the national economy, and 29 per cent. in large-scale industry.

This increase in the number of workers will be obtained, apart from the natural increase in population, in two ways, firstly, by drawing a larger number of women into all branches of the national economy, the aim of the Soviet authorities being to make woman completely independent economically from the men-folk of her family. Wages for the same class of work is the same for women as for men, and married women are encouraged to enter into and to continue their employment by the provision of efficient scientifically conducted day-crèches and kindergartens for children, and by the organization of factory, institution, and public dining-rooms as well as public laundries, &c. Secondly, it is expected that the organization of large-scale agriculture and its mechanization will set free a large number of peasants who will find employment in industry.

The total wages fund in 1937 is to increase by about 19 milliard roubles as compared with 1932, i.e. by 55 per cent. for the national economy as a whole and by 64 per cent. for large-scale industry.

Real wages are to be doubled ; it is hoped to effect an increase of two and a half times in the norms of consumption of such products as meat, fats, fish, eggs, sugar, and industrial goods.

Expenditures on social insurance and State appropriations for disability and old age pensions, health and cultural services for non-agricultural workers is to increase from 4·3 milliard roubles to 9·3 milliard roubles, an increase of more than 100 per cent. in the five years.

The number of workers in urban and rural areas, served by the communal kitchens and dining-rooms by 1937, is to be two and a half times the number so served in 1932 ; in the towns alone some 32·7 millions of people are to be catered for.

The Home Trade.

In order to facilitate a rise in the standard of living of the people it is, of course, necessary not only to increase the output of consumers' goods, but also to improve the flow of supplies of such goods both in the towns and villages. Accordingly the Plan estimates :

An increase of the home trade by 2·5 times, from 31·9 milliard roubles in 1932 to 80 milliard roubles in 1937 (in 1932 prices), accompanied by an increase of 2·5 times in the output of articles of general consumption by the light and food industries.

An increase of the retail State and co-operative trade system by 37 per cent. and its technical reconstruction.

A reduction of the average level of retail prices by 35 per cent. as compared with 1933 prices.

The Plan estimates an increase in the national income from 45·5 milliard roubles in 1932 to 100 milliard roubles in 1937 (i.e. more than doubling the income during the five years), with an increase of the fund available for the national consumption by 2·4 times accompanied by an enormous growth of capital accumulations in the socialized economy, as well as an increase of State reserves.

Among the social services which very materially affect the standard of life of the workers are the health services, municipal works (housing, sanitation, lighting, &c.) as well as pre-school care of children and education, with all of which we now propose to deal briefly.

Health.

During the First Piatiletka, the health services had already made great progress. The number of beds in hospitals had increased by 65 per cent., the number of health centres had increased 3·5 times, the number of workers enjoying a holiday at rest-homes had more than doubled.

During the Second Piatiletka there is to be an extensive application of sanitary preventive measures, an increase of the expenditures on health protection, workers' rest, and physical culture from 5·4 milliard roubles in the First Five-Year Plan to 19·6 milliard roubles in the Second. A rise in the number of hospital beds in the cities by 44 per cent. and in the villages by 98 per cent.

About 423,000,000 roubles are to be invested in the construction of new hospitals in the towns. This will provide 7·2 beds per 1000 of population (exclusive of special sanatorium accommodation for patients suffering from tuberculosis, nervous diseases, &c.) as compared with 5·9 per 1,000 in 1932. In the most important industrial centres the proportion will be higher.

There is also to be an extensive development of medical aid provided for the rural population. About 220,000,000 roubles are to be spent in the construction of hospitals in the rural areas and the provision of hospital places in the latter will increase from 0·8 per 1,000 of population in 1932 to 1·5 per 1,000 of population in 1937.

Considerable attention is to be paid to the organization of new and the re-equipment of existing first-aid stations in various parts of the Union. The number of such stations attached to enterprises are to be nearly doubled during the five years.

Numerous new rest-homes and sanatoria of all kinds are to be built, particularly children's sanatoria and hospitals.

There are to be large investments in the organization of new and the extension and improvement of existing medical schools and research institutes, the manufacture of pharmaceutical preparations and medical apparatus and instruments.

Some 275,000,000 roubles are to be spent on developing the health resorts, and the number of persons taking their holidays at rest-homes is to increase from 914,000 or 40·3 workers per 1,000 insured in 1932 to 2,034,000 or 75 per 1,000 workers insured in 1937.

Expenditure on maternity and infant welfare in 1937 will be about two and a half times that in 1932, whilst help for incapacitated workers and pensions for families who have lost their bread-winners, will also be more than doubled.

It is proposed to invest about 260,000,000 roubles in the construction of public baths of various kinds as against 102,000,000 roubles so invested in the First Five-Year Plan. The capacity increasing from accommodation for

422,150,000 visits per annum in 1932 to a possible 887,700,000 visits in 1937.

A considerable sum is also to be spent on public wash-houses, the proportion of the town population served by them increasing from 1·9 per cent. in 1932 to 13·6 per cent. in 1937.

A wide campaign is to be waged amongst the population to inculcate sanitary hygienic habits—for this purpose popular hygiene and sanitary institutes have been and are being organized.

Housing and Municipal Services.

Capital investments in municipal, housing, and cultural construction in the Second Five-Year Plan is estimated at about 32 milliard roubles, including 13·4 milliard roubles on housing, 6·2 milliard roubles on urban municipal services, 3·1 milliard roubles on education, and 2·9 milliard roubles on health protection. Expenditure on municipal services include the extension of the water supply, sanitation, omnibus, and tramway services, &c.

It is estimated that the above-mentioned expenditure on housing will result in about 33 per cent. increase in the dwelling accommodation of the U.S.S.R., exclusive of the additional accommodation provided for commercial and hotel purposes.

Whilst considerable investments are to be made in increasing housing accommodation in the large towns, such as Moscow, Leningrad, Kharkov, Kiev, Sverdlovsk, &c., the Plan is so constructed as to provide very rapid rates of housing and municipal development in the more backward national Republics and in the new industrial areas.

Special investments are to be made in rural housing with the aim of providing family dwellings with separate baths, common dining-rooms, wash-houses, crèches, &c., similar to those in urban areas.

The number of towns with a central laid-on water supply is to increase from 366 in 1932 to 440 in 1937. This will mean that all towns with populations above 10,000 to 15,000 will have laid-on water. The number of towns with a sewage system will increase from 55 to 125, all towns with over 50,000 population being provided with such a system.

The number of towns with tramways is to increase from 50 to 70 (the length of tramway line increasing from 2,870 kms. to 5,000 kms.)   The number of tramways is to increase from 8,000 to 15,000.

The towns with bus services will increase from 117 in 1932 to 200, the number of buses increasing from 1,400 to 7,200, and it is estimated that the passengers carried will increase from 300,000,000 in 1932 to 1,500,000,000 in 1937.

A taxi service is to be established in forty towns, some 7,000 new taxis being brought into exploitation.

Amongst other projected expenditure may be mentioned some 850,000,000 roubles for road building, 633,000,000 roubles for the supply of electricity, gas, and central heating, and 124,000,000 roubles for the provision of green spaces, public gardens, &c., in the towns.   There is also to be considerable expenditure on the arrangement of Parks of Rest and Culture, the organization of pleasure bases at spots suitable for excursions on the workers' rest days, &c.

Population in Urban and Rural Areas.

It is estimated that the population of the U.S.S.R. will increase from 165,700,000 on January 1, 1933 to 180,700,000 on January 1, 1938.

The population of the towns increased rapidly during the First Piatiletka, and it is estimated that during the Second Piatiletka it will increase by some 6,300,000 souls, partly as a result of the natural increase of population, and partly by the migration of people from the rural to the urban areas.

On the other hand, in view of the mechanization of agriculture and the general transformation of living conditions in the rural areas, there will also be an opposite influx from the towns to the villages.   It is calculated that the towns will supply the villages with about a million trained workers and experts of all kinds, educated in the factory training schools and in the technical and higher educational institutions, and if the families of these workers be included, the rural population will increase at the expense of the towns by at least 1,500,000 people.

It should, of course, be noted that already during the First Piatiletka and still more during the Second Piatiletka, the face of the village and the type of its inhabitants has changed and is changing fundamentally.

Agriculture is being industrialized and agricultural workers are becoming more and more akin to industrial workers. The amenities of the towns—good schools, theatres, cinemas, clubs, libraries, hospitals, &c., are being introduced to a greater and greater extent in the villages.

EDUCATION

Illiteracy was practically eliminated in the course of the First Piatiletka. The Second Five-Year Plan is to put the final touches to this elimination and to organize the further education and training of the now literate but still little educated amongst the adult population, particularly in the villages and in the more backward national Republics of the U.S.S.R.

With regard to the system of children's education, the Plan provides for the more rapid extension of the universal compulsory seven-year course of polytechnical school education in the rural areas (in the towns this is already practically universal), and the extension of the poly-technical schools with a ten-year course.

The schools are divided into three groups : I. for those eight to eleven years of age; II. for those twelve to fourteen years of age, and III. for those fifteen to seventeen years of age. The first group provides elementary education ; the second and third, secondary education.

It is estimated that by 1937 all children in the Soviet Union, eight to eleven years of age and 90 to 92 per cent. of those twelve to fourteen years of age, will be provided with school accommodation, whilst about 50 per cent. of town children completing the first and second groups will be enabled to pass into the third group. In industrial towns and in workers' settlements the proportion of children enabled to attend schools with a ten-years' course (eight to seventeen years of age) in 1937 is estimated to reach about 70 per cent.

The increase in the number of children in the various

groups in the urban and rural areas will be seen from the following table :

	1932. (in thousands.)			1937. (in thousands.)		
	Urban.	Rural.	Total.	Urban.	Rural.	Total.
1st Group'(8–11 years of age)	3,458	14,622	18,080	3,466	14,828	18,294
2nd Group (12–14 years of age) . .	1,369	2,208	3,577	2,521	8,047	10,568
3rd Group (15–17 years of age) . .	53	4	57	828	239	1,067
Total .	4,880	16,834	21,714[1]	6,815	23,114	29,929

It should be noted that in 1914 there were less than 8,000,000 children in the elementary and secondary schools of the Russian Empire.

The average operative expenditure per pupil is estimated to increase from 40·3 roubles in 1932 to 64·5 roubles in 1937 in the first group ; from 113·5 roubles to 173·6 roubles in the second group ; and from 145·3 roubles in 1932 to 295·7 roubles in 1937 in the third group.

It is estimated that the total number of pupils (in elementary and secondary schools, workers' faculties, factory apprenticeship schools, universities, and technical colleges) will be 36,000,000 in 1937, as against 24,200,000 in 1932, i.e. 197 persons per 1,000 inhabitants against 147 persons per 1,000 inhabitants in 1932.

The number of clubs and club-like institutions (Trade Union clubs, houses of culture, cottage reading-rooms, &c.) is scheduled to increase from 49,300 (5,900 in the towns and 43,400 in the villages) in 1932 to 76,900 (6,300 in the towns and 70,600 in the villages) in 1937. The

[1] [NOTE.—In 1932 there were in addition about 99,000 pupils in special schools for juveniles over twelve years of age who had been unable to attend elementary schools.]

number of Trade Union clubs and clubs belonging to the Commissariat for Education alone is to increase from 6,800 (4,090 in the towns and 2,710 in the villages) in 1932 to 10,870 (4,520 in the towns and 6,350 in the villages) in 1937. The number of circulating libraries is estimated to increase from 15,000 in 1932 to 25,000 in 1937.

A great expansion of the periodical press, book publications of all kinds and of the theatre, cinema, art exhibitions, &c., is also provided for in the Plan.

At the present time there are in the U.S.S.R. 8 scientific academies, 737 scientific institutes, with 152 branches of All-Union or Republican importance, 43 central scientific laboratories, 60 All-Union and Republican museums, 10 very large libraries, 9 observatories, and a large number of local scientific research institutes of all kinds in all branches of the national economy. An additional 13 scientific institutes and 7 branches of institutes are to be organized during the Second Piatiletka, but attention is to be mainly focussed on improving the work of the existing institutions.

During the Five-Year period it is proposed to spend a total of 22,400,000,000 roubles on general education; 24,400,000,000 roubles on the training of skilled workers and specialists for the various branches of the national economy ; 4,020,000,000 roubles on the advancement of science ; 890,000,000 roubles for art, &c.

The special attention paid in the First Piatiletka to the extension of education, the press, and culture generally amongst the more backward national minorities inhabiting the U.S.S.R., is to be continued throughout the Second Piatiletka, the aim being to raise the culture of these non-Russian minorities to the level attained or to be attained by that part of the population known as the Great Russians.

Pre-School Care of Children.

Partly in the interest of the children themselves, and partly in order to place woman on an economic equality with man, by giving her an opportunity to enter into any sphere of the national economy and public work she may desire or may be fit for, the Soviet system has always paid very special attention to the pre-school care of children.

With this object in view, expectant mothers receive six to eight weeks' leave of absence, with full wages, before and after child-birth. Lying-in hospitals are provided, and on the birth of the infant an allowance is made for its layette, as well as a special allowance of milk for the nursing mother ; time off is given for nursing the baby during working hours, or where the mother cannot nurse the child, a special allowance is made for the food of the latter.

Day-crèches for infants up to three years of age have been organized in connexion with a large number of industrial enterprises, as well as in the villages for agricultural workers.

During the Second Piatiletka there is to be an increase in the number of places in day-nurseries by 164 per cent. in the cities and 129 per cent. in the villages.

By 1932, 60 per cent. of the women workers' children were provided with accommodation in crèches ; by 1937 it is expected that nearly the full 100 per cent. will be so covered.

The kindergartens and other pre-school institutions provided accommodation for 5,200,000 children in 1932. In 1937, some 16,000,000 children are estimated to attend them.

In the rural areas a large proportion of the kindergartens and other pre-school institutions are seasonal, in order to free the mothers for the necessary field work during the sowing and harvesting seasons.

Thus, in 1932, there were 420,000 children in the permanent and 3,682,000 children in the seasonal crèches and kindergartens in the rural areas. In 1937 it is estimated that there will be accommodation for 1,812,000 children in the permanent and for 11,261,000 children in the seasonal pre-school institutions in the rural areas.

The number of children in the various children's homes was 217,000 in 1932, and is expected to increase to 330,000 in 1937.

In the towns some 80 per cent., and in the villages about 70 per cent., of the children of pre-school age will be accommodated in pre-school institutions.

Operative expenses on pre-school institutions will total about 1,533,000,000 roubles.

WILL THE SECOND FIVE-YEAR PLAN SUCCEED ?
ACHIEVEMENTS IN 1933 AND 1934

It will be seen from the foregoing that the Second Five-Year Plan envisages an enormously increased development of the national economy of the U.S.S.R.—the question naturally arises as to what hope there is that this great programme will be fulfilled.

The reply is that, in the first place, the First Five-Year Plan, the amplitude of which was no less tremendous, was, in the main, fulfilled in four and a quarter years.

Secondly, although the estimates for 1933, the first year of the Second Five-Year Plan, were not quite fulfilled, this was mainly due to the lag in output at the beginning of the year. After the first quarter there was an almost steady improvement month by month as the Soviet workers gained experience and mastered the technique of the newly constructed works.

Actually in 1933 large-scale industry showed a gain of 8·8 per cent. over 1932. The increase for producers' goods amounted to 10·4 per cent. and for consumers' goods to 6·7 per cent. The gains recorded by the coal and steel industries, which formerly were among the most backward, were well above the average for all industries.

Coal production, at 75,837,000 tons, was 19·5 per cent. above that of the proceeding year, whilst pig-iron, at 7,133,000 tons, and steel ingots, at 6,852,000 tons, showed increases of 15·8 and 15·5 per cent. respectively, over the preceding year.

Production of automobiles and tractors showed especially large gains. The output of motor cars and lorries, totalling 49,753 cars, increased 86 per cent., and that of tractors, 78,263, an increase of 46 per cent. Power output in 1933 totalled 15·9 milliard kilowatt-hours, recording a gain of 17·9 per cent.

In the textile industry growth was uneven. Output of cotton cloth totalled 2·6 milliard metres, a gain of 8 per cent. over 1932. Production of wool cloth amounted to 119 million metres, one-third greater than the preceding year.

The new branches of the textile industry—silk and knitted goods have made exceptional progress. Silk goods, until recently considered a luxury product, are now in wide demand. The silk mills produced a total of 24 million metres, an increase of 23·5 per cent. over 1932. The knitted goods industry as a whole recorded a growth of 14 per cent., while certain branches, such as hosiery and outer garments, showed a gain of about 25 per cent.

The output of the light industries run by the Commissariat for Light Industry amounted in 1933 to 8 milliard roubles, i.e. 200 million roubles more than in 1932. This is almost twice the output at the beginning of the First Piatiletka, and two and a half times the pre-war production.

Speaking at the December 1933–January 1934 session of the Central Executive Committee of the U.S.S.R., Mezhlauk, then Vice-Chairman of the State Planning Commission (Gosplan) of the U.S.S.R., referred to the early failures of the new enterprises constructed in the U.S.S.R. and said :

> ' The year 1933 has been a turning-point, some of the most complex enterprises constructed on the most modern principles . . . of mass production have been mastered by our people to such an extent that not only was it found possible to work them to full estimated capacity, but even to exceed the latter. As examples may be mentioned the Stalingrad Tractor Works ; the Moscow Ball-Bearing Works ; Furnace No. 1 of the Azov Steel Works ; No. 3 of the Magnitogorsk Works ; Furnace No. 7 of the Dzershinsky Works ; the Berezin and Gorlovka Chemical Works, &c.
>
> ' The production of synthetic ammonia and nitrogen fertilizers has been successfully accomplished and the plan of output overfulfilled.   The Volkhov Aluminium Combine, after a long and difficult struggle with " infantile diseases," has, since the second half of 1933, come out strong and healthy and is now working to full projected capacity and even exceeding it.'

Similarly, Molotov, Chairman of the Council of People's Commissaries, said :

' The increase in the output of industry does not yet guarantee the complete fulfilment of the plan of increase in production. But the special feature of 1933 has been the steady increase in output from quarter to quarter. During the first months of the year, the output of the heavy industries was even somewhat below that in the corresponding months of 1932. But subsequently we succeeded in attaining a far more rapid rate of progress of industrial output. . . . This was particularly the case as regards the output of coal, oil, metals, &c., during the second half of the year.'

It naturally took and takes some time to master the new works, especially as the number of well-trained skilled workers was, and still is, insufficient, but as the number of such workers increase, so the period required to set an enterprise into smooth operation tends to diminish.

As regards agriculture, the good harvest of 1933 is well known (the gross yield was 898,000,000 centners as against 698,700,000 centners in 1932 ; 835,400,000 centners in 1930 ; and 801,000,000 centners in 1913), but it is particularly important to note that the good meteorological conditions in 1933 would not have been sufficient to account for this high yield. The following were very important contributing factors :

The early sowing period. In 1933, 25,000,000 hectares were sown as early as March and April as compared with only 15,000,000 hectares sown in March and April 1932. Only 14,000,000 hectares were sown in the latest month for sowing.—June 1933—as compared with 21,500,000 hectares in June 1932.

The better quality of ploughing. Weeding on a large organized scale—millions of hectares were freed from weeds in 1933.

Other factors which have had an important influence in raising the harvest were extra early-sowing and fallow ploughing, and an increased use of both animal manure and artificial fertilizers. The gathering in of the harvest, stacking, threshing, &c., were all better done in 1933 than in 1932. In general, all branches of agricultural work was on a far higher level in 1933.

7

By December 15, 1933 (two to three months earlier than in 1932), the plan of State grain collection, i.e. the sale by the kolkhozy and individual farmers of fixed quantities of grain to the State at a fixed price, was completed.

Similarly, the accumulation of seed grain by the kolkhozy for the following year's sowing proceeded far more rapidly in 1933 than in 1932. By the end of December 1933 many areas had already stored a sufficiency of seed grain, and in other areas they had nearly completed their seed accumulations ; the kolkhozy, as a whole, had by that time accumulated 52,000,000 centners of seed grain, whereas by the same date in 1932 they only had 22,000,000 centners of seed grain stored.

The preliminary returns for the first six months of 1934 show a further very distinct advance in the national economy of the U.S.S.R.

The value of the gross output of the heavy industries January–June 1934 was, according to preliminary returns, 9,400,000,000 roubles or 28 per cent. in excess of that during the corresponding period of 1933, whilst the number of workers employed increased by 10·2 per cent.

It is further interesting to observe that the output in the first six months of 1934 was actually in excess of that in the whole of 1930 (9,087,000,000 roubles).

About 47 to 48 per cent. of the annual plan of the heavy industries was fulfilled during the first six months of 1934. Never before had such a high proportion of the annual plan been fulfilled during a corresponding period. In the first six months of 1933 only 42 per cent. of the year's plan had been fulfilled, and in 1932 only 35 per cent.

The following table shows the output of some of the more important products of the heavy industries in January–June 1934 and 1933 respectively :

Product.	Output January–June 1933.	Output January–June 1934.	Excess of Output in 1934 over 1933 (percentage).
Coal (thousand tons) .	34,672	44,021	26·9
Oil (exclusive of gas) (thousand tons) . . .	9,978	11,845	18·7
Oil drilling (metres, thousands) . . .	368	645	75·2
Coke (thousand tons) .	4,631	6,640	43·4
Iron ore (thousand tons) .	6,318	9,430	49·3
Pig-iron (thousand tons) .	3,173	4,910	54·7
Steel (thousand tons) .	3,027	4,491	48·4
Rolled metal (thousand tons)	2,271	3,090	36·1
Copper pyrites (thousand tons) . . .	595·1	995·9	67·4
Aluminium (tons) . .	1,100	5,834	430
Locomotives for railways, calculated as " E " type (number) . . .	415	552	33·0
[1] Goods trucks (calculated as two-axle, number) .	8,499	12,605	50·7
[1] Motor lorries (number) .	17,463	23,438	34·2
[1] Motor cars (number) .	2,260	7,662	239·0
[1] Tractors (Stalingrad and Kharkov Works, number)	30,105	38,515	27·9
Tractors (Chelyabinsk Works, number) . . .	21	3,174	—
Sulphuric Acid (thousand tons) . . .	246·0	339·9	35·8
Superphosphates (thousand tons) . . .	318·7	433·9	36·1
Ammonium sulphate (thousand tons) . . .	10·2	41·1	304·4

In all the above industries the productivity of labour has increased, and the cost of production has decreased in 1934 as compared with 1933.

Numerous enterprises completed their six months' plan by the middle of June 1934. The most important soap works in the U.S.S.R. report their output of household and toilet soap January–June 1934 as being in excess of the total output for the whole of 1933.

[1] To June 20 of each year.

Particularly interesting and important is the progress made in the ferrous metals industry, the more so since in previous years this branch had lagged considerably behind the plans. During the first six months of 1933, the daily output of pig-iron varied from 15,000 tons to a little under 22,000 tons, but in 1934 there was an almost steady increase in the daily output from 22,000 tons to over 30,000 tons, indeed, on June 27, 1934, the output reached 31,986 tons or 6·1 per cent. in excess of the plan for that day. The output of steel in 1933 varied from 15,500 tons to 19,000 tons, but in 1934, with a very few ups and downs, output increased from about 22,000 tons a day on January 1, 1934, to over 27,000 tons in June. On June 27, 1934, the output was 27,853 tons or 99·5 per cent. of the plan for that day.

The output of rolled metal showed a similar increase, and on June 27, 1934, the output was 19,807 tons or 99 per cent. of the plan.

The gold industry completed its six-months plan by June 26, 1934, the quantity of gold produced being 51 per cent. in excess of that in the corresponding period of 1933.

Similarly, in the first five months of the current year the Soviet food industry increased its output, as compared with the same period last year, by the following amounts : meat, 117,000 centners ; sugar, 1,050,000 centners ; vegetable oil, 4,880,000 centners ; soap, 709,000 centners ; salt, 2,010,000 centners ; dairy products, 279,000 centners ; sweets, 378,000 centners.

The total output of the food industry increased by 18·7 per cent. or by 375 million roubles (in 1926–7 prices) as compared with the same period last year. The turnover of the communal kitchens increased by 42 million roubles.

Conspicuous improvement in the work of the food industry during this period, particularly in May, accounts for the great increase in output. For the first time it closely approached fulfilment of the monthly plan (97·1 per cent. in May). The May programme was over-fulfilled in many branches of the industry ; in the sugar industry by 263·4 per cent. ; fruits and vegetables, 167 per cent. ; in the dairy industry, 23 per cent. ; and soap and oil production from 6 to 7 per cent.[1]

[1] Since the above was written, final returns have been issued for the output of industry in the first half of 1934. The gross value of

The work of the railways has also improved as compared with the first half of 1933, but not to the same extent as the heavy and a number of other industries, the position as regards transport is consequently still very difficult.

As for agriculture, the spring sowing has been carried out at rates hitherto unknown in the U.S.S.R.

By May 1, 1934, a total of 36,229,000 hectares had been sown as compared with 25,320,000 hectares by May 1, 1933.

Even in 1930, when the climatic conditions were exceptionally favourable, the total area sown by May 1, was not more than 33,000,000 hectares.

By June 15, 1934, a total of 94,342,000 hectares had been sown or 1·5 per cent. in excess of the spring sowing plan. By June 15, 1933, the spring-sown area totalled 90,655,000 hectares.

The kolkhozy sowed 71,230,000 hectares (4·7 per cent. above their plan) as compared with 66,411,000 hectares by June 15, 1933.

As an insurance against drought extra-early sowing has been carried out in the spring of 1934 over an area of nearly 4,000,000 hectares, whilst about 1,000,000 hectares has been sown with sprouted seeds. As soon as drought conditions in the Southern areas became apparent, a number of measures were taken, such as the utilization of mountain torrents and other sources of water for artificial irrigation purposes, ditches were dug, swampy land was sown with various grains and fodder, crops hit by the drought were resown, &c. Weeding, fallow ploughing, &c. have been carried out on a large scale.

Much scientific work has been and is being done in

the output of industry, as a whole, in January to June 1934, was 17,813·6 million roubles (in 1926–27 prices), i.e. 19·7 per cent. in excess of the output of industry in the corresponding months of 1933. The value of the output of the means of production was 10,870·9 million roubles or 26·5 per cent. in excess ; Production of Consumers' Goods, 6,942·7 million roubles or 10·6 per cent. in excess ; Heavy Industry, 9,515·8 million roubles or 29·3 per cent. in excess ; Timber Industry (lumber, furniture, paper, matches), 1,183·5 million roubles or 8·6 per cent. in excess ; Light Industry, 4,172·3 million roubles, or 3 per cent. in excess ; Food Industry, 2,392·0 million roubles or 23·3 per cent. in excess of the corresponding months of 1933.

The output during the first six months of 1934 is now stated to have been 46·1 per cent. of the annual plan.

connexion with agriculture. Particularly interesting is the work done by the Institute for Artificial Rain in Turkmenia ; located in the dryest spot of the whole Soviet Union, in Ashkhabad, it is surrounded by the hot Turkmenian sands. This Institute conducted a series of experiments throughout the spring, during which it succeeded in regularly precipitating passing clouds by sprinkling them with chemicals from aeroplanes.

Within five to seven minutes after the plane passes, a line of lighter colour appears on the cloud which spreads till the whole cloud is milky white, while underneath appears a dark zone of falling rain. The first drops that fall are small and impregnated with the chemical, but these are followed by normal drops of rain.

The scientists of the Institute therefore consider that, in the very near future, when the weather forecast says 'cloudy, possible showers,' it will be possible to correct this when necessary to 'cloudy and we shall make rain.'

In addition, by burning certain chemicals which precipitate the normal moisture always present in the atmosphere, the Institute has succeeded in creating an artificial dense fog in Ashkhabad on a bright day in May. This fog lasted for four hours. It is hoped to produce such a fog in the form of a cloud and then precipitate it as rain, thus the artificial production of rain on a sufficiently large scale would seem now to be within the realms of possibility.

The herds of livestock began to diminish seriously in 1929, although in 1933 the decrease was far less than in previous years, and there was even an increase in the number of pigs from 11,000,000 heads in 1932 to 12,200,000 in 1933. But 1934 has shown a distinct advance, and particularly such important stock-breeding areas as Uzbekistan, Eastern Siberia, the Ukraine, &c., report considerable improvement.

It is evident from the above facts and figures that the infantile diseases which attacked various branches of the Soviet national economy in the early stages of the organization of a large-scale highly technical industry and large-scale collective farming are being eradicated. There are, of course, and there are still likely to be a number of ups and downs, but the 'ups' are steadily increasing and the 'downs' decreasing, and as the Soviet workers gain more skill and the members of the kolkhozy become more accustomed to collective farming and slowly shed their individualist psychology, so the amplitude of progress is likely to become steadily wider and more sweeping.

There can therefore be little doubt that, providing there is no armed attack upon the U.S.S.R., the Second Five-Year Plan will be, in the main, successfully completed.

CONCLUSION : POSSIBILITIES OF SOVIET MARKET

There can be very little doubt that with the successful completion, in the main, of the Second Five-Year Plan the U.S.S.R. will become, if needs be, economically independent of other countries. Does this signify that from 1937 onwards she will no longer form an important market for other industrial countries generally or for Great Britain in particular ? We have already dealt with this question briefly in the Introduction, but it may be as well to wind up our analysis of the Second Five-Year Plan with a little further discussion of the possibilities of trade with the U.S.S.R.

In the first place, we would stress here once again the fact that when a country becomes industrialized it by no means follows that her imports decrease. We will take as instances the three countries which have made the most striking industrial progress during the last quarter of the nineteenth century and the early (pre-war) years of the present century. In a booklet entitled *Sheltered Markets*, Mr. McDougall makes some very interesting points in this connexion. As regards the U.S.A., Mr. McDougall states :

> ' In 1870 the United States was still a country whose most important interest was agricultural production. British capital was rapidly developing the great railway systems and industrial production had already become of great importance, but the export of wheat, meat, cotton, and other foodstuffs and raw material was still the source of the greatest wealth to the Republic. In that year the total value of the goods imported into the United States was 435 million dollars. In 1913, the total value of United States imports was 1,813 million dollars ' [page 21].

And the share of Great Britain in these imports rose from 151·4 million dollars in 1870 to nearly 272 million dollars in 1913.

Similarly, between 1882 and 1913 'the value of German imports increased from 3,000,000,000 marks to 10,000,000,000 marks' [page 22], and the share of these German imports supplied by Great Britain increased from 378 million marks to 810 million marks in 1913.

As for Japan, in 1873 'the total value of Japanese imports was 28 million yen, and in 1913, the value had increased to 729 million yen' [page 30], and the quantity of these imports supplied by Great Britain increased from 11·9 million yen to nearly 122·5 million yen.

The competition for foreign markets between all countries has become more and more acute, particularly since the World War, but the industrialization of any country and its economic development generally has for the most part been accompanied by an increased demand for all sorts of goods in that country. There is no reason to think that the U.S.S.R. will form an exception to this rule.

On the contrary, in so far as the aims of the economic system of the U.S.S.R. is not the making of individual private profit, but the raising of the standard of life and culture of every one of her huge population, the demand for all classes of goods by her people is increasing far more rapidly than her own industry can possibly supply for a very long time.

Possibly the character of her imports as also of her exports may alter with the development of her national economy, but for a long time to come Soviet imports are likely to remain mainly manufactured and semi-manufactured goods. However, the economic development of the U.S.S.R. resulting from the First and Second Five-Year Plans and from succeeding Five-Year Plans—for the U.S.S.R. will undoubtedly continue to *plan* her economic development—has undoubtedly increased her bargaining power as a customer.

During the First Five-Year Plan, the Soviet Union was forced to import equipment and raw materials from other countries on most onerous terms and often at unduly high prices, and in order to pay for them she had to export much foodstuffs and raw materials which she would have preferred to use at home.

Now, however, and still more in a few years time she will be in a position to say to would-be sellers, ' It is more convenient for us to purchase such and such machinery and other goods from you, but if you cannot or will not sell your goods to us at a fair price and on reasonable terms then we shall do without them or manufacture them ourselves.'

The position of the U.S.S.R. on this question is well summed up in an article by M. Rosengoltz (Commissar for Foreign Trade) in the Russian journal *Bolshevik*, May 31, 1934, from which it may be of interest to give some extracts here. In the course of this article M. Rosengoltz says :

> ' During the 16 years of the existence of Soviet Russia, 1918–1933, our imports amounted to the huge sum of 8·4 milliard roubles . . . the State monopoly of our foreign trade has made it possible to direct our imports exclusively in the direction of the importation of the means of production on which we spent no less than 7 milliard roubles or nearly 85 per cent. of our expenditure on imports, 3·3 milliard roubles being spent on equipment.
>
> ' The Soviet machine construction industry, built up with the aid of these imports, now has an output 10 times that of pre-war—nearly all the machinery required by the U.S.S.R. is now manufactured in the Soviet works and there is no machine which we could not, if needs be, manufacture at home.
>
> ' During the First Five-Year Plan we invested 50 milliard roubles on capital constructions and imported 2 milliard roubles' worth of foreign equipment. The Second Five-Year Plan provides for the investment of 133 milliard roubles on capital constructions and if the same relative amount of equipment were to be imported we should have to spend over 5 milliard roubles, but we are now in a position to carry out the Second Five-Year Plan with a very small quantity of foreign importations.'

Turning to the question of the prospects of future Soviet imports and the economic relations of the U.S.S.R. with other countries, M. Rosengoltz says :

' We do not stand for autarchy, but we shall make no large purchases unless the conditions are radically improved. If long term loans are offered to us at normal rates of interest we shall certainly consider them and increase our imports, but we shall not agree to undue high prices and high interest charges on credit such as we paid in the past.'

After pointing out the healthy financial position of the U.S.S.R., the way in which, as a result of the State Monopoly of Foreign Trade, the Soviet Government has been able to regulate its exports and imports in such a way as to assure the possession of sufficient valuta to meet her full commitments, and the fact recognized on all sides of the meticulous way in which the U.S.S.R. had met all her financial obligations, M. Rosengoltz continued :

' During the period of the First Five-Year Plan, the U.S.S.R. has achieved enormous successes in the regulation of its commercial relations with the capitalist countries. She has, among others, concluded trade agreements and treaties with France, Britain, Latvia, and Greece, prolonged her trade agreements with Italy and Estonia, regulated and improved the trade agreements with Persia, concluded a commercial treaty with Turkey, and developed new forms of economic relations with that country. During this period diplomatic relations have been established with the United States, which may promote the development of trade relations between the Soviet Union and that country. Diplomatic relations have been restored with Spain and Uruguay.'

M. Rosengoltz then pointed to the fact that Soviet-German economic relations had worsened, but that Soviet relations with Italy were normal, whilst they had greatly improved with France. With regard to relations with the U.S.A. and Great Britain, he said :

' For a number of years our purchases in the U.S.A. were fairly large. In 1929 our imports from the U.S.A. amounted to 177 million roubles, with an adverse trade balance against us of 134 million roubles ; in 1930 the figures were 264 million roubles and 223 million roubles respectively, and in 1931 229 million roubles and 207 million roubles.

' Our exports to the United States met with all sorts of obstacles and restrictions. They even restricted the importation of Soviet gold used to pay for commodities which we purchased in the United States. At the same time normal credit terms were not accorded us in America.

' All these circumstances naturally affected our trade with the United States. We could not tolerate a continuation of such abnormal trade relations with America or reconcile ourselves to a system of trade that was benefiting the United States alone. Now, however, the position has improved considerably.

' Soviet orders have been very essential to many important branches of British industry. Exports of British engineering products in 1931 amounted to 33 million pounds sterling, of which the share of the U.S.S.R. was 4·4 million pounds.

' In 1932 exports of machinery from Great Britain fell to £29·5 millions, of which £7·5 million or over 25 per cent. went to the U.S.S.R. The export of machine tools to the U.S.S.R. exceeded 80 per cent. of their total export from Great Britain.

' In 1932 the U.S.S.R. held first place in the British export of electrical machinery and boilers, the Soviet Union having taken 25 per cent. of the total British exports of these commodities. In 1932 the U.S.S.R. occupied the 7th place in British exports as against the 16th in 1930.'

After referring to the blow at British-Soviet trade resulting from the British embargo and the Soviet counter-embargo imposed April–July 1933, M. Rosengoltz dealt with the new Anglo-Soviet Commercial Agreement and stated :

' The new Anglo-Soviet Trade Agreement signed on February 16, 1934, makes it possible to develop economic relations with Britain provided, of course, that the necessary conditions are created in Britain ruling out the possibility of a recrudescence of new obstacles to the development of trade between the two countries.

' The primary object of the new trade agreement is, over a term of several years, to equalize the balance of payments between the two countries. Since an agreement has been reached I feel certain that our business organizations will do everything possible to ensure the execution of the provisions regarding the balance of payments. We sincerely hope that business circles in Britain will grant the U.S.S.R. as favourable conditions (credit charges, credit terms, prices) as we enjoy in other countries, and will thereby stimulate our purchases in Britain.'

There can be no reason whatever for doubting that the U.S.S.R., however much it may develop economically and become industrialized, will still maintain a demand for a large variety of products, many of which Great Britain could certainly supply.

Point is added to this argument by the following statement made by the Glasgow Correspondent of the *Financial News* (July 9, 1934) :

' Since the trading agreement concluded with the U.S.S.R. by this country, Russia has been one of the best overseas markets for British iron and steel goods.

' The contracts received cover a variety of products, structural and boiler plates, sections, sheets, tubes, and manufactured products, including locomotives.

' In the first quarter of this year, Russia actually consumed about twice as much British steel as Canada, the Russian imports totalling about 30,000 tons.

' The Soviet Union is now the largest manufacturer of iron and steel in Europe, and, if the Second Five-Year Plan is successful, production in 1937 will be about twice the British record, reached in 1929.

' *Since the per capita consumption is still very low, however, expert opinion believes that Russia will provide*

a great market for steel for many years. The consumption per head per annum works out at a little
over 100 lb. This is only one-third of the British
figure and one-tenth of the American record achieved
in 1929.' (Our italics.)

The same is, of course, true for many other articles which
we can export to the U.S.S.R.

But Anglo-Soviet trade will never reach really satis-
factory proportions until the premiums charged for
guaranteeing Soviet bills are very much reduced, and
Soviet bills are discounted by the banks at normal rates.

It cannot be too strongly urged that if a new chapter
in Anglo-Soviet trade is to be opened, the terms upon
which credits are guaranteed should be radically revised
and the period for which they are granted considerably
prolonged.

As a result of the Agreement concluded in February 1934,
there has already been a welcome increase in Soviet orders
placed in Great Britain, and the recent reduction of the
charges for credit guarantees should do something to
stimulate Anglo-Soviet trade—but there is still far too
much hesitation, far too much unjustified apprehension of
imaginary risks involved in trade with the Soviets.

We certainly 'missed the boat' in regard to the
enormous imports made by the U.S.S.R. in connexion with
the First Five-Year Plan. It is to be hoped that we shall
not repeat the mistake in regard to the Second and
subsequent Five-Year Plans by undue timidity and
procrastination.

The Soviet Government is, and will certainly continue
to be, far more than solvent.

As a customer, the credit of the Soviet Government
stands high not only because they have so far met punctu-
ally all their financial obligations, but because the State
monopoly of foreign trade signifies that the U.S.S.R. can
so plan her imports and exports as not to permit her
commitments to outrun her resources, and behind the
Government stands the illimitable wealth and resources
of a sixth of the world's surface.

III

TABLES SUMMARIZING FIVE-YEAR PLAN ESTIMATES

I

INDUSTRY—OUTPUT [1]

	1913.	1928.	1932.	(Preliminary Returns) 1933.	Estimate 1937.
Total output (million roubles), at 1926–7 prices . . .	16,253 [3]	18,300	43,300	46,800	92,700
Electrical energy (million kw. hours)	1,950	5,000	13,400	15,900	38,000
Coal (thousand tons) . .	29,040	35,220 [2]	64,310	75,837	152,500
Oil and gas (thousand tons) .	9,234	11,651 [2]	22,272	22,519	46,800
Benzine and ligroin (thousand tons)	156	882 [2]	2,881	2,655	8,550
Kerosene (thousand tons) .	1,521	1,912 [2]	3,560	3,862	7,800
Peat (thousand tons) . .	1,688	5,200 [2]	13,302	13,210	25,000
Pig-iron (thousand tons) .	4,216	3,283 [2]	6,173	7,133	16,000
Steel (thousand tons) . .	4,231	4,251 [2]	5,922	6,852	17,000
Rolled metal (thousand tons) .	3,506	3,408 [2]	4,289	4,904	13,000
Copper (thousand tons) . .	32·3	30·1	46·6	45·3	155·0
Lead (thousand tons) . .	1·3	2·6	18·8	13·7	120·0
Zinc (thousand tons) . .	2·9	2·2	14·8	16·9	100·0
Aluminium (thousand tons .	—	—	0·92	4·4	80·0
Locomotives (number) . .	654·0	580·0	828	1,008·0	2,800
Freight cars (number) . .	14,832	10,868	22,300	—	118,400
Motor cars and lorries (number)	—	671 [2]	23,879	49,753	200,000
Tractors (number) [4] . .	—	1,272 [2]	50,640	78,263	167,000
Tractors (thousand h.p. . .	—	22·0	774·4	—	—
Combines (number) . .	—	—	10,010	8,578	20,000
Sulphuric acid (thousand tons).	121·3	194·7	494·6	570·1	—
Superphosphates (thousand tons) (14 per cent.) . . .	62·9	155·4	613·8	688·8	3,400
Rubber tyres (number in thousands) . . .	19·2	84·4 [2]	552·5	678·0	3,000
Rubber footwear (million pairs)	27·9	37·7	64·8	62·3	120
Leather footwear (million pairs)	8·3	29·6 [2]	82·0	76·6	180
Cement (thousand tons) . .	1,438	1,850	3,489	2,749	7,500
Paper (thousand tons) . .	23·8	295	471	508	1,000

[1] Where the figures for 1937 in this table differ from those in the table of preliminary estimates (Table III, p. 115), they are the revised figures.

[2] 1927–8.

[3] Output at pre-war prices 8,430 million roubles, the index for conversion to 1926–7 prices is the one used by the Supreme Economic Council of the U.S.S.R. for 'Producers' Prices,' i.e. 1913 = 100 ; 1926–7 = 192·8.

[4] Calculated as 15 h.p. each.

8

II

ESTIMATED VALUE OF CAPITAL CONSTRUCTIONS AND OF ENTERPRISES SET AND TO BE SET INTO OPERATION DURING THE FIRST AND SECOND FIVE-YEAR PLANS (MILLION ROUBLES AT 1933 PRICES)

	First Five-Year Plan (1928–9–1932).		Second Five-Year Plan (1933–7).	
	Value of Capital Constructions.	Value of Enterprises set into Operation.	Value of Capital Constructions.	Value of Enterprises set into Operation.
I. Industry . . .	24,789	15,728	69,475	68,980
Including:				
Group 'A' [1] . .	21,292	13,214	53,402	53,514
Group 'B' [1] . .	3,497	2,514	16,073	15,466
II. Agriculture . .	9,687	9,234	15,239	15,379
Including:				
Sovkhozy . .	4,475	4,250	5,475	5,510
Machine tractor stations . . .	1,173	1,135	6,360	6,425
III. Transport . . .	8,933	7,723	26,522	25,743
Including:				
Railways . .	6,398	5,550	17,464	17,320
Water . . .	1,189	975	4,396	3,833
Motor road . .	1,100	1,000	3,455	3,410
Civil aviation .	246	198	1,207	1,180
IV. Communications .	565	495	1,679	1,700
V. Exchange and distribution . .	943	900	1,679	1,701
VI. Cultural and social administrative [2] .	5,585	4,506	18,806	18,527
Total .	50,502	38,586	133,400	132,030

[1] 'A' includes Producers' goods. 'B' includes Consumers' goods.
[2] Not including expenditure for these purposes by industrial and other enterprises.

III

PRELIMINARY ESTIMATES [1] OF ANNUAL OUTPUT OF SOME OF THE PRINCIPAL PRODUCTS UNDER THE SECOND FIVE-YEAR PLAN AND ACTUAL OUTPUT IN 1932

	1932.	1933.	1934.	1935.	1936.	1937.
All industry (million roubles, 1926-7 prices) . . .	43,300	46,900	55,800	67,800	82,500	102,713
Electrical energy (million kw. hours) .	13,390	15,855	19,000	24,000	30,000	38,000
Coal (million tons) .	64·31	76·69	96·25	110·0	126·60	152·50
Oil and gas (million tons) . . .	22·27	23·02	30·66	35·0	40·50	47·50
Benzine and ligroin (thousand tons) .	2,881	2,758	3,000	3,650	5,550	8,550
Kerosene (thousand tons) . . .	3,560	4,000	4,964	5,150	6.000	7,800
Peat (million tons) .	13·30	13·15	18·00	21·0	23·0	25·0
Iron ore (thousand tons)	12,063	15,100	21,800	27,250	31,725	36,900
Manganese ore (thousand tons) .	830	1,040	1,700	2,000	2,3000	2,700
Ferrous metals (million roubles, 1926-7 prices) . . .	1,303·6	1,561·0	2,081·2	2,440·0	3,025·0	3,750·0
Non-ferrous metals (million roubles, 1926 7 prices) .	572·2	564·7	722·2	889·0	1,277·0	1,732·0
Machine construction and metal working (million roubles, 1926-7 prices) .	9,211·0	8,281·0	9,747·0	11,720·0	14,095·0	17,100·0
Including :						
Motor tractor industry (million roubles, 1926-7 prices) . .	600·0	1,008·0	1,380·0	1,600·0	2,000·0	2,575·0
Transport machinery (million roubles, 1926-7 prices) . .	811·6	880·0	1,176·0	1,545·0	1,920·0	2,480·0
Agricultural Machinery (million roubles, 1926-7 prices) . .	345·0	370·0	465·0	570·0	625·0	665·0
Electro - technical industry (million roubles, 1926-7 prices).	1,099·2	1,194·0	1,410·0	1,710·0	2,110·0	2,650·0
Turbines (thousand kws.) . . .	226	405	810	1,300	1,350	1,400
Generators (thousand kws.) . . .	966	731	924	1,250	1,350	1,400

[1] Some of the estimates have since been revised, but the final revised figures for the separate years not yet being available, we give the preliminary figures of the Plan throughout this table (see Note 1 to Table I, p. 113).

8*

III—(continued)

	1932.	1933.	1934.	1935.	1936.	1937.
Motor cars and lorries (number in thousands) . . .	23·9	49·5	72·0	110·0	140·0	200·0
Tractors (thousand h.p.) . . .	774·4	1,240·0	1,730·0	1,888·0	1,992·0	2,500·0
Combines (number in thousands) . .	10·0	10·6	12·0	18·4	24·0	25·0
Bicycles (number in thousands) . .	128·4	140	320	400	530	700
Radio receiving sets (number in thousands) . . .	29·3	30	150	300	500	700
Chemical industry (million roubles, 1926–7 prices) [1] . .	1,497·1	1,620·0	2,044·0	2,752·8	3,568·8	4,510·7
Superphosphates (14 per cent.) (thousand tons) . . .	614	690	900	1,624	2,822	3,400
Phosphorous flour (thousand tons) .	396	430	535	1,300	2,000	2,900
Rubber footwear (million pairs) . .	64·8	61·6	65·0	75·0	95·0	120·0
Tyres (number in thousands) . . .	552·5	705	1,500	2,000	2,500	3,000
Building materials (million roubles, 1926–7 prices) [2] . .	494·5	490·6	680·5	867·8	1,021·4	1,226·7
Timber industry (million roubles, 1926–7 prices) . .	1,799·5	1,787·7	2,065·4	2,458·1	2,946·2	3,643·0
Paper (thousand tons) .	471·2	508·0	600·0	655·0	740·0	1,000·0
Textile Industry (million roubles, 1926–7 prices) .	4,301·3	4,600·8	5,227·8	7,005·0	9,616·3	13,932·5
Soap (40 per cent.) (thousand tons) .	357·2	295·0	460·0	600·0	850·0	1,300·0
Gramophone records (number in millions)	1·7	3·0	7·0	15·0	25·0	40·0
Scientific and cultural necessities (million roubles, 1926–27 prices) . .	261·3	302·2	348·2	424·0	570·7	822·5
Photographic and cinema products (million roubles, 1926–7 prices)	58·1	80·9	118·0	154·2	219·0	300·0
Industries under Commissariat for Supply (million roubles, 1926–7 prices) .	4,634·7	4,836·5	5,906·4	7,568·8	9,846·4	13,100·0
Including :						
Meat . . .	720·4	648·4	862·0	1,225·0	1,750·0	2,476·0
Fish . . .	261·0	285·0	359·0	413·0	510·0	570·0
Sugar (granulated) . .	249·5	332·0	422·5	511·0	632·0	840·0
Conserves . .	104·4	115·0	129·6	230·3	270·0	380·0
Tobacco . .	208·6	221·9	239·9	302·0	344·0	487·0
Kitchen factories .	155·0	202·5	250·0	325·0	425·0	550·0

[1] Not including rubber.
[2] In enterprises under Commissariat for Heavy Industries alone.

IV

AGRICULTURE

(1) AREA UNDER CULTIVATION
(Million Hectares)

	1913.	1928.	1932.	(Preliminary Returns) 1933.	Estimate. 1937.
Total	105·5	113·0	134·4	129·7	140·0
Including grain total .	94·4	92·2	99·7	101·5	104·8
Winter wheat . .	31·65 {	6·2	11·8	10·8	14·4
Spring wheat . .		21·6	22·7	22·4	26·4
Rye (Spring and Winter) .	—	24·6	26·2	25·4	23·7 (Spring)
Industrial plants .	4·6	8·6	14·9	12·0	14·1
Including :					
Cotton . . .	0·69	0·97	2·17	2·05	2·24
Flax (long fibre) . .	1·02	1·36	2·51	2·40	2·4
Sugar-beets . .	0·65	0·77	1·54	1·21	1·5
Oil seeds . .	2·00	—	7·98	5·79	6·4
Fodder . . .	2·1	3·9	10·6	7·3	11·6
Vegetables . . .	3·8	7·7	9·2	8·6	9·6

(2) CROPS OF MOST IMPORTANT CULTURES
(Million Centners)

	1913.	1928.	1932.	1933.	1937.
Total Grain . .	801·0	733·2	698·7	898·0	1,048·0
Wheat (Winter) }	212·0	215·0	202·5	277·3	397·5
Wheat (Spring) }					
Rye (Winter) . }	231·0	192·0	220·3	241·9	272·5
Rye (Spring) . }					
Barley . . .	110·0	55·0	50·3	78·5	84·0
Oats . . .	147·0	165·0	112·4	154·1	191·5
Cotton (unginned) .	7·4	8·22	12·7	13·2	22·6
Flax . . .	4·5	3·52	5·0	5·6	8·0
Sugar-beet . .	109·0	101·4	65·6	90·0	276·0

(3) USE OF MACHINERY IN AGRICULTURE

	1913.	1928.	1932.	1933.	1937.
Tractors (at end of year) 1,000 h.p. [1] (thousands) .	—	278·1	2,225·0	3,100·0	8,200·0
Combines (number in thousands) . . .	—	—	14·1	25·0	100·0
Motors and engines at end of year (thousands) .	—	—	7·9	20·1	170
Gross value of agricultural produce (in million roubles, 1926–7 prices) . .	14,200[2]	14,500[3]	13,072·0	—	26,566·0

[1] Allowing for depreciation.
[2] At pre-war prices the value was 10,200 million roubles. To convert to 1926–7 prices the index used was 1910–4 = 100 ; 1926–7 = 139·3.
[3] 1927–8.

IV—(continued)

(4) SOVKHOZY AND KOLKHOZY [1]

	1928.	1930.	1932.	(Preliminary Returns) 1933.	Estimate. 1937.
No. of Sovkhozy (at end of year)	3,125	—	10,203	—	—
Sown area (thousand hectares)	1,735	—	13,557	14,107	15,800
No. of Kolkhozy (thousands) .	33·3	—	211·05	224·5	—
No. of farms collectivized (millions)	·417	—	14·9	15·196	—
Percentage of total number of farms in U.S.S.R. . .	1·7	—	61·5	65·0	100
Area sown (million hectares) .	1·367	—	91·6	93·858	120·5
No. of machine tractor stations (at end of year) [2] .	—	637	2,446	2,660	6,000

[1] June 1 of each year.
[2] There were no Machine Tractor Stations in 1928.

V

FINANCE

(1) NATIONAL INCOME

	1913.	1928.[1]	1932.	(Preliminary Returns) 1933.	Estimate 1937.
National Income (milliard roubles 1926–7 prices) .	21·100[2]	24·3	45·5	50·0	100·0
State Budget Revenue (milliard roubles) . .	3·25[3]	6·9	30·51	39·2	—
State Budget Expenditure (milliard roubles) . .	3·25	6·75	30·28	36·0	—

[1] October 1, 1927 to September 30, 1928.
[2] The National Income in 1913 was 14·025 milliard gold roubles ; to convert this into 1926–7 prices, we have added 50 per cent. of the 1913 gold value.
[3] Gold roubles : the National Income is given in 1926–7 prices, but the budget figures are in the prices of the corresponding years.

(2) FINANCING NATIONAL ECONOMY

(MILLIARD ROUBLES, 1933 PRICES)

	1932.	Estimate 1937.	Total during Second Five-Year Plan.
Financing national economy . . .	30·4	44·7	208·2
Including :			
Capital investments . . .	19·2	24·0	114·2
Increase in current capital . . .	4·1	5·8	26·4
Expenditure on administration and defence	2·5	4·3	19·0

(3) PLAN FOR FINANCING SOCIAL AND CULTURAL MEASURES

(INCLUDING CAPITAL INVESTMENTS, OPERATIVE EXPENSES, &C., IN MILLIARD ROUBLES, 1933 PRICES)

	1932.	Estimate 1937.	Total during Second Five-Year Plan.
General education	2·57	6·34	22·40
Training of experts, &c.	3·21	6·18	24·40
Science	0·47	0·97	4·02
Art	0·08	0·25	0·89
Press	0·08	0·14	0·66
Health and physical culture . . .	2·11	5·62	19·63
Labour protection, &c.	1·72	2·66	11·25
Total .	10·24	22·16	83·25

VI

LABOUR

(1) NUMBER OF WORKERS (Thousands).

	1928.[1]	1932.	(Preliminary Returns.) 1933.	Estimate 1937.
Number of Wage Workers[2]				
total . . .	11,599·0	22,601.3	21,882·8	29,641·0
Total employed in industry . .	3,534·0	6,728·8	—	9,411.0
Large-scale industry alone . . .	3,126·0	6,302·6	5,997·3	8,832·0
Construction . }	723·0	3,125·8	2,345·0	3,425·0
Transport . . .	1,365·0	2,222·0	2,116·0	2,806·0
Communications (Post, Telegraph, &c.) .	—	224·3	241·5	336·0
In railway transport alone . . .	971·0	1,526·0	1,396·0	1,696·0
Education . . }		1,347·2	1,480·5	2,065·0
Art . . . } 1,888·0		84·5	—	123·0
Health . . }		647·2	711·0	1,020·0
Trade . . .	—	1,410·8	1,497·0	2,285·0
Public dining establishments . .	—	515·1	549·0	860·0
Agriculture, forestry, and fishing . .	2,007·0	4,097·1	—	5,070·0
Machine tractor stations and State Farms	345·4	2,474·1	2,474·0	—

(2) WAGES

	1928.[1]	1932.	(Preliminary Returns.) 1933.	Estimate 1937.
Wages (Average for the year, roubles)—				
All branches of the National Economy	703·4	1,427·0	1,567·0	1,748·0
Industry . .	843·1	1,410·1	1,519·0	1,769·0
Large-scale industry	870·0	1,466·6	1,641·0	1,843·0
Construction . .	996·0	1,509·0	1,622·0	1,794·0
Railway transport }		1,496·0	1,613·0	1,860·0
Communications } 855·0		1,333·0	1,424·0	1,655·0
Education . }		1,633·0	1,730·0	1,960·0
Health . . } 665·0		1,248·0	1,413·0	1,560·0
Trade . . .	—	1,351·0	1,351·0	1,533·0
Public dining establishments . .	—	1,059·0	1,085·0	1,200·0
Forestry . . .	—	1,094·0	—	1,291·0
Agriculture (Sovkhozy and machine tractor stations) .	327·4	866·0	1,074·0	1,260·0
Total Wages Bill—				
All Branches of National Economy (millions) . .	8,158·8	32,737·7	34,279·9	51,808.6

VI—(*continued*)

(3) WOMEN WORKERS (AT END OF YEAR)

	1932.		1937.	
	Number. (thousand.)	Percentage of Total Workers Employed.	Number. (thousand.)	Percentage of Total Workers Employed.
Total in National Economy	6,819·3	29·9	10,140·4	33·9
Including :				
Industry . . .	2,335·0	33·8	3,635·0	37·0
Building . . .	437·8	16·1	561·0	17·6
Transport . .	293·2	13·3	464·4	16·4
Public dining-rooms .	363·4	64·7	650·0	69·0
Education . .	795·5	55·5	1,271·0	58·0
Health . . .	475·7	70·7	776·0	73·0
Agriculture . .	556·4	23·9	823·0	27·5

[1] In 1928 real wages were nearly 40 per cent. in excess of 1913.
[2] The number of workers includes both manual and brain workers, but not domestic workers and occasional day-workers.

VII

POPULATION

(MILLIONS AT END OF YEAR)

	1913.	1928.	1932.	(Preliminary Returns) 1933.	Estimate 1937.
Total . . .	139·3	154·2	165·7	168·0	180·7
Including :					
(a) Urban . .	24·7	27·6	38·7	—	45·0
(b) Rural . .	114·6	126·6	127·0	—	135·7

INDEX

For Product Safety Concerns and Information please contact our EU
representative GPSR@taylorandfrancis.com
Taylor & Francis Verlag GmbH, Kaufingerstraße 24, 80331 München, Germany

www.ingramcontent.com/pod-product-compliance
Ingram Content Group UK Ltd.
Pitfield, Milton Keynes, MK11 3LW, UK
UKHW021826240425
457818UK00006B/93